Even If It Was

F R E E

**Rediscover
the human
side of
buying and
selling
technology**

PAUL RUSSELL

Cover illustration by Emma Cowley
Instagram.com/ditsydoodlesdesign

For Sam, Joe, Alice

ABOUT THE AUTHOR

Early in my working life I looked after mysterious machines humming and flashing away in goldfish bowl rooms. My dad, an electrician, was proud that I finally got my hands dirty on the 'tools' and together would spend happy hours discussing how computers and the internet worked.

From connecting machines together, my career moved into consultancy and sales channels, bridging the gulf between technological innovation and business results. Increasingly I shifted from technology outputs to human outcomes with AECOM (formerly URS Corporation) and Ricoh. My time with Microsoft's Partner Advisory Council in Seattle was one such learning experience of how 'big tech' sees the debate between value driven technology and business growth.

I have been fortunate to travel widely meeting inspirational people curious to challenge status quo and technology's role in change for good. And when the Internet of Things (IoT) shift began to take hold I joined the grand masters of scale at IBM. A time spent pushing boundaries of human-centred design through an appreciation of what matters to people. Finally, I will never forget my days at Servo, a small technology company based in the picturesque Derbyshire Dales, memorable for long hours, lifetime mates, and baptism into what the saying - *'we are all in sales'* - meant.

And now to this book.

Paul Russell.

CONTENTS

A WORD ON THE TITLE

"We all have a blind spot, and it is shaped exactly like us."
- JUNOT DIAZ

My mouth must have been as wide open as a frog. What we had just heard from our prospective customer left us speechless. He should have signed the contract. We had won the deal and the champagne was on ice. We had dotted every 'I' and crossed every 't.' So be told *'even if it was free I'm not signing'* was something else. We weren't selling timeshares or Ponzi schemes; the deal was a bona fide corporate transaction for technology. Free Guy as I will refer to him, was a serious business leader; with no interest in playing games. So this conversation was something quite different and definitely not taught at sales school.

Whilst others left incredulous I was more curious to find out what was behind his words. And after a career meandering between hundreds of conversations of value and outcomes through technology, I came to realise the problem was us. It was just that we didn't know it.

The conversation

My book is about conversations we have with people like Free Guy. People who disrupt our status quo thinking and demand us to think differently. Something we furiously claim we do already but on reflection may secretly admit we don't.

Like a switch going off in my head his words flipped me from being a technologist into someone else. A revelation that whilst I had a passion that technology was an incredible force for change, I began to realise the human factor was being overlooked from the selling side of the conversation. A nagging thought that despite an abundance of all things innovative and at times jaw-dropping, human outcomes were being compromised.

So this book is for those who have suffered disappointment from the selling and buying conversation and is intrigued to see if there is a better way to go about it.

The superpower within us all

We make up to 35,000 conscious decisions a day. What should I wear to work, what's for dinner or can I fit in a run later. Choices that we make that are a mix of impulse, reason and prioritisation. And avoidance. Nearly forgot that one! And when we consider problem solving our way through this 35k number, we turn to technology increasingly to help us navigate, calibrate and automate our decision-making. All done to reduce how our brain has to work and reserve energy for more complex events that may occur. Must mention sleep because that is a huge influence on all of this. Says someone who thought it was smart to run on few hours to demonstrate how on top of things I was.

In this book I will refer to this as being our inner Converger and Diverger. When we converge on a problem that needs resolution we will lock down on what we see relying on assumptions and biases to support our theories and decisions. When we diverge we turn on our curiosity and vulnerability radar to explore and experiment with what we think is going on. If it were a colouring book when we converge we colour between the lines, when we diverge there are no lines.

It might seem strange to say but to exercise our Diverger mindset takes courage. As children our world was all about curiosity and vulnerability exercising our Diverger skills with joy and abandonment. A time of exploration and experimentation where no question was silly and the answers encouraged more questions - 'why parent, why teacher, why world?' But as adults and in the business context it takes courage to go outside the lines. An attribute that is not easy to live with, but as beautifully put by artist, Henri Matisse, *"to look at something as though we have never seen it before requires great courage."*[1]

When we turn on our Diverger radar it is like having a superpower that can help ourselves and others unlock their approach to the problems they face. These characteristics I am referring to - Converger and Diverger - will dovetail throughout the book, as I stitch together the pros and cons of how we use these cognitive skillsets with each other.

Turmoil of free

Would you turn down for free something you know you needed and could afford? Something that you knew would influence your outcomes and experiences? Something that evidence suggested you needed now not later? A contradiction that makes no sense when everyone knows there is a price to pay, a bill to be settled and compensation expected for efforts made.

Free Guy was in turmoil. His industry - engineering and construction - was going through a change in direction and he was committed to pushing his business ahead of its competitors. This was not one of those 'technology-led change initiatives' that seem to last for perpetuity. No, this was a transformation event where the only outcome worth talking about was how people would contribute to sustainable growth. One has everything to do with the inevitability of change, the other about human vulnerability and curiosity.

It's all a game

Business is measured in absolute terms. A game that we are all playing with winners and losers offering little wriggle room for creativity when the 'chips are down.' A game that the Converger in us knows only too well. It is why we do what we do - and what others expect of us. But a game that can make us overconfident we are on the winning side only to find that we are being blindsided by our bias and illusion.

This human frailty that translates into business fragility is a hard thing to talk about for many. Deep down we may individually acknowledge this, but outwardly keep our foot to the metal at all costs. Not because we are being reckless, but because we fear others will judge such thinking as weak or slow.

When we converge we are using our brain's analytic function. A place of logic, blueprints and rationale that we frequent enormously. It is our default master system where stereotyping biases live. People will describe this as our 'hardwired' state of mind. Whereas when we diverge we touch our brain's empathic functional network where intuition, stories, empathy, and moral reasoning reside. But our brains are being exhausted with the focus on doing what's next. As Daniel Kahneman, a famous American psychologist puts it, *"We simply do not have the real estate in our heads to be constantly open."* [2]

Imagine a two-way mirror

Look one way and we see technology helping us deliver results, hit targets, and achieve goals. A world led by technocrats who promote confidence and certainty that technology helps us to be more predictable than before. And why not? This is exactly what humankind has been doing since, forever. A world where our inner Converger thrives. A world dictated by speed, aided and abetted by technology, and driven by the pressures of winning the game.

Yet when we look the other way, the mirror shows us a complicated and complex landscape of fear, uncertainty, and doubt over the best way to solve our problems. An experience that chips away at our ability to understand what is going on and where the solutions we put forward are at odds with the social outcomes we aspire to. A world where our inner Diverger is desperate to shine but is often diffused by the pressures of 'colouring within the lines' of business life.

It's not our fault

Technology might well be the ultimate modern seduction. Whether it is a free app to help organise a forthcoming house move or an expensive digital platform to connect suppliers and customers, we are all in some way or another tempted by what technology offers. Why? Because in our conscious mind we need tools to help us make our lives easier. And in fairness to the criticism of modern-day technology, this phenomenon has been with us for a lot longer than we may think. The word itself - technology - comes from the Greek meaning 'the way things are gained.' A transliteration of two words - 'techne' (art, skill, craft) and 'logos' (saying, expression) that underlines what might be getting lost when we talk about humans and technology.

When faced with a new challenge we attach both rational and irrational markers to what success should look like. We measure this through our stated outcomes - *'did we move house successfully'* or *'did we achieve promised growth through the market we created?'* And we will either create finite indicators of progress or rely on our gut. And for those selling and buying technology, the pressure to commit to tangible outcomes is right up there. Often at the expense of the irrational thoughts rattling around in that part of the brain that doesn't do logic and reason.

Today's world, supported by **innovative** technology, appears to have no limits encouraging us to be more **confident** that we can **speed** up our ambition to achieve more. An ever-increasing circle, that I call a Trilogy of Temptations, feeding our insatiable desire for instant gratification. Why wait if we can have it now? A characteristic hiding deeper problems that are less about choices and costs of 'technology,' even if free, and more about how we talk to each other.

The book's structure

The book is written in two halves. In the first half, I explore the trilogy of temptations and how our inbuilt unconscious biases and illusions of knowledge suggest as Convergers we know more than we do. And then in the second half, I set out to rediscover our inner Diverger's mindset of curiosity and intrigue to understand our problems better. A set of skills squeezed out by the ding dong of 'business as usual' that ironically stifles the creativity and imagination we need to survive and thrive. Be assured I am not going down any neuroscientific route, but I will talk at times about brains and feelings - you are warned! You will also stumble across Hints. A series of tactics, some mine some borrowed, that as you read I will encourage you to pop into what I am calling a Divergers Toolkit. Nothing too formal, just ideas.

My storytelling friends

And threaded throughout are stories from a wonderful group of storytellers who add colour to my theme. An eclectic group of people who share their personal stories of inspiration and vulnerability to challenges influenced by technology. I cannot thank them enough for their patience and guidance throughout.

Belinda Rushton, Dan Brown, Mike Bugembe, Linda Chandler, Karan Navani, Catherine Coale, Doug Field, Debbie Ward, Sharon Richardson, Mark Williams, Viktoria Vrbiniak, Paul Finnis, Isobel Rimmer, Carolina Souviron, Ann Longley, David Mantock, Vicky Reddington, Matthew Marson, Sean Crichton-Browne, Claire Penny, Jason Betteridge, Lewize McCauley Crothers and Catherine Russell.

One more thing

I would like you to pause and think about something in your life - personal or professional - that you would consider to be your innovative thing. Something that makes you feel productive, collaborative, or quite simply, happy. It might be an analogue thing or a digital thing; it might be big or small, free, or otherwise. I only ask that it has to be designed and manufactured by another human being; nature has the label for the ultimate innovation.

CHAPTER 1

TRILOGY OF TEMPTATIONS

"If you're ready to give away what's most precious to you, you may be amazed at what the world gives back."
- CHRIS ANDERSON

When a US senator asked Mark Zuckerberg, Facebook CEO, *"how do you sustain a business model in which users do not pay for your service,"* the gaping divide between value and outcome was laid bare. The question was raised during the investigation into the Cambridge Analytica data leak in 2018. Zuckerberg's reply to the senator that day was breathtakingly simple when he replied, *"We run ads."* [3] A blunt exchange that exposed the juxtaposition of two diverse perspectives. One person offered something for free but knew it was not, and the other not knowing what they did not know. One person was fully immersed in how to monetise human interaction, the other was puzzled about where and how.

Technology is such a fluid word that it appears as free as air; a bit like an unexpected dividend. Whilst to others, it feels expensive and oversold; like an unwelcome tax bill. So anytime the word 'free' pops up in a conversation our hormones go crazy, allowing irrational thoughts to shape our behaviour. The Sunday morning car boot sale or the £1 store pulls us into buying something even when we don't need it. An inexplicable guilt trip where it seems plain wrong not to buy something. Or a feeling that we will be missing out if we don't; is free Wi-Fi still a crowd pleaser?

The business world, however, is not a massive fan of giving anything away for free, where the rule of the game is one of compensation. To be found peddling anything for free may be career-threatening and where even the free lunch has disappeared under a cloud of anti-bribery regulation and governance procedures.

Tech makes us feel great

Levon Helm's lyrics, *"Feelin' good, feelin' good, all the money in the world spent on feelin good,"* [4] could have been the anthem for the technology industry. We spend our money on tech in the firm belief that we will feel better and a lot smarter than we were before. Your innovative idea I mentioned at the start might just be the best thing since 'sliced bread.' Indeed, it might be sliced bread. Something you would continually invest in - at any price. And where the manufacturers know you will too! Whilst all of this 'tech love fest' encourages us to believe we can go faster, be more competitive and win bigger, there lurks a fear. A feeling that what is desirable, viable and feasible to us is becoming harder not easier to obtain. A paradox that our decision-making might not be as sound as we thought and that the outcomes we crave might not be as forthcoming as we expect. Or is this not the case? Haven't we also played the game of ping pong on investment versus outcome? Or are we now sceptical of the return-on-investment (ROI) models and total cost of ownership (TCO) calculations so prevalent not too long ago?

Slow down or speed up?

The irony is that just as we are advised in mainstream media to slow down, be mindful and detox from our screens, the technology we buy encourages us to speed up and grab what we can. The dichotomy of speed - *slow down to think clearer, speed up to keep ahead* -increasingly points to the usefulness of technology as a trusted tool. The inextricable desire to go faster comes from our ancestors, where fight or flight would activate their sympathetic nervous system to most likely, run away from danger. And in business, many find slowing down counter-productive and sluggish. And can you blame them especially when the tech is at hand to make them go faster - and faster?

The die was cast when we realised in the 1960s that we could pack increasingly smaller transistors onto pieces of silicon that would power our phones, cars, and businesses. This scenario supported the belief that if technology doubles in speed every two years - known as Moore's Law - our aspirations and goals could grow accordingly.[5] Such an evolution in our approach to technology now means we buy everything as a commodity fuelling the 'we want it now' societal urge. We can not only have our 'cake and eat it,' but at a price, we can afford - or free - that allows us to think bigger and faster!

Bumps in the road

When Facebook went offline in late 2021, people were shocked to realise that when one system went down, so did others. Suddenly a network of interconnected pieces we took for granted was inexplicably unavailable, and we had no control over getting it back. And I do not just mean the public internet side of our lives - I mean how businesses connected with customers, suppliers, and workers. A veritable house of cards, and it felt like no one had told us this might happen. Except for the fearmongers and dystopian naysayers of course. Access was denied, and the computer was saying no.[6] And then in 2021 the largest cargo ship in the world, ran aground in the Suez Canal, throwing delicate just-in-time supply chains into disarray - semi-conductor chips for cars and phones, perishable goods for high street shops and even garden gnomes for the UK gardening fraternity. [7]

Like space invaders in the arcade game, these unexpected bumps in the road come at us from all angles - and seemingly get faster. When we are 'slowed' down by such unexpected events, like digital networks going offline or cargo ships running aground, we naturally seek ways to avoid being caught out again. I cannot speak about a Plan B for garden gnomes, but in the context of the Suez Canal incident, we are now witnessing 'smart' technology being used to build 'captainless' ships. Why invest in a human crew when artificial intelligence, onboard cameras, and predictive data analysis can safely get goods from A to B without the need for people? [8]

Be careful what you wish for

Let me ask you a question - three in fact - that can apply equally to your personal and business life.

- Has the quest for speed, like next-day delivery of goods or instant access to information reduced the complexity of managing your time and relationships at work or pleasure? Yes, no or it depends?
- Are you confident more than ever that technology is giving you better protection against the bumps in the road ahead when things go wrong? Yes, no or does it still depend?
- Do you feel more in control of things that matter to you because of how you use technology to help you get what you need? Yes, no, or still undecided?

Amazon and others would no doubt say a firm yes to all three of my deliberately closed questions. But what if I reframed those questions into just one - *'how might you use technology in the future to create an experience that responds better to your ever-changing world.'* Is it now a lot harder to give an absolute yes or no answer, perhaps making you think more about the practicalities and implications of how technology might help in the future? But isn't the truth that technology is helping us make better decisions and reduce the bumps in the road? Have we become so immersed in technology being part of everyday life that we have stopped noticing when the bumps appear and disappear? Computer viruses used to be a real pain (they still are to be fair) and could shut down businesses for days. But that significant bump has now surely gone, right? Or the 'cheque is in the post' delay syndrome? That bump has gone also now we are all digital. Yes? And what about when the Y2k bug threatened to bring banks and aeroplanes crashing down? We don't have the dystopian threat of computers crashing anymore. Is this correct or do we have 21st-century bumps in the road that are more cynical and destructive?

Uncertain times

As a youngster, I have a vivid memory of a TV advert advising my parents on what to do when a nuclear bomb detonated over our heads in Birmingham, UK. I remember it being quite scary. But if the unthinkable did happen, my dad would simply take interior doors off their hinges and create a makeshift shelter weighed down by heavy suitcases.[9] Futile or a clever distraction? Because at the time, this was in the 1970s, there was a clear and present danger of nuclear attack - or so said the UK Government.

And when the Cold War ended in the early 1990s a popularised acronym popped up, known as VUCA. A time that heralded a shift in thinking that the world was becoming more volatile, uncertain, complex, and ambiguous than ever before.[10] We might remember Y2K, the Wall Street crash and more recent contenders - cost of living, military conflict, mental health, and climate change. VUCA is here to stay. Rather than removing the bumps in the road, we are seeing more of them appear, like a massive game of global Whack-A-Mole, that we seem to be losing. And whilst some of the problems we experience are inherently complex, outside of our control and too big to comprehend at times many others sit within our circle of influence. When a crisis is caused by poor judgement, lack of accurate information or failure of trust, our lives seem to exist in a VUCA bubble. In the words of Michael Blastland, our futures are *"reminiscent of chaos and a warning to those who think they know how this will play out: uncertainty needs only an inch to take a mile."* [11]

And if our desire for speed is our tactic to escape from these turbulent bumps we are witnessing, what does this do to our understanding of *'what does good really look like'?*

Dogs Behaving Oddly From Ottawa

What? I will explain, I promise.

Look at your smartphone. You most likely have one to facilitate an experience, whether for work or pleasure. Do you care about how the product was conceived, designed, and built? Are you bothered about the intricacies of the electronics stuffed inside? Or the efforts of designers and engineers who painstakingly built the user interface of screens and buttons with you in mind? And are you remotely interested in the regression testing performed to make the software work every time - even after you have dropped it in the bath? And why should you? You are only interested in positive consequences for you, whether free or not, not how they were designed or built.

I call this <u>DBOFO.</u> Or more imaginatively, <u>Dogs Behaving Badly From Ottawa</u>. It is a mnemonic that I use as a framework to highlight where things might be going amiss with our technological prowess, leaving the human outcomes out in the cold. We all know that to move past obstacles, humankind would <u>design</u> and <u>build</u> a tool to help overcome the problem, make the tool easy to <u>operate</u> and achieve the <u>function</u> we needed to perform. All done to get us to the <u>outcome</u> we envisaged.

Your innovative thing

I love the Spotify™ app. For me, it does what it says on the tin, and I am happy to pay for it. Why? Because it triggers three emotions in my mind. Firstly, I have a solution to listen to the music I like on my terms. Second, it is viable in terms of the impact financially and finally, it is feasible because I have a platform to maximise my enjoyment - a smartphone, Wi-Fi and internet. Spotify passes my DBOFO test with flying colours. Spotify holds 'retained value' waiting for me i.e., playlists, recommendations - personalised for me.

Spotify has been <u>designed</u> with me in mind, <u>built</u> to work with what I have, <u>operates</u> and <u>functions</u> as I like and gives me the positive <u>outcome</u> I want. And for the price that suits my wallet. For me (Spotify + DBOFO = experience) adds up nicely. But then, if a bump in the road appears such as repeated loss of service, price hike or ethical curve ball, my loyalty will be tested. And what if we think scale which is where Free Guy was sitting?

The 21st-century hospital is considered an asset designed from the bottom up with clear goals and objectives with technology being increasingly part of the 'build.' Initially, digitally designed and increasingly prebuilt for offsite efficiency and zero carbon compliance. And then subsequently, packed with layers of technology to support and enhance patient, visitor, and staff experience. A connected system of systems that promises positive social outcomes for the local community, reducing operational costs and maximising real-time insights. What is there not to applaud here?

But what if death rates go up, not down, queues get longer, not shorter, and the general feeling from the community is negative towards the project? Somewhere along the time-sensitive stages of DBOFO, something has gone wrong. It might be culture, design fault, poor planning, or an external event, like a pandemic, which raises a question mark against the outcome the community expects. Or the root cause might be an individual architect's interpretation of the vision or a sub-contractor substituting inferior components due to problems in the supply chain. Such events will likely span decades to reveal themselves or happen overnight. Either way, the positive outcome fades for the community and significant workarounds are needed to be found to recover confidence.

This is DBOFO where the outcome becomes so negative it undermines the entire vision and execution. And for hospitals, you could replace them with high-speed railways or kitchen extensions. Or scissors if you are left-handed. Like me. And as you digest the DBOFO theme I am suggesting you might also be wondering what a mnemonic is. So I ask you to consider, *'My very excited mother just served us nine pies.'* [12] Which will help you remember the order of the planets, closest to furthest from the sun. FYI - Mercury, Venus, Earth, Mars, Jupiter, Saturn, Uranus, Neptune, and Pluto. Such knowledge might be helpful when doing the crossword or taking part in a pub quiz. But be warned. Recently Pluto was demoted to dwarf planet status, so look out for that trick question.[13]

Systems of systems

Our lives at work and play are increasingly intertwined in a spaghetti of connections, each with unique languages, rules, and protocols that mysteriously harmonise when we tap, swipe and click on our computers. We work hard to design build and operate these systems to function as single entities, thus protecting us, the consumer, from the individual parts. Systems where resilience is refined to smooth out bumps in the road, even when one component, node or link fails, deliver expected outcomes at all times. But of course, systems have been around for a long time. The cuneiform writing system from Mesopotamia (now Iraq) around 320BC is an example, and so are the sewage systems, first designed in India and Pakistan during 3300 BC. [14] Examples of human ingenuity to solve complicated problems that we still use today. I doubt whether those that follow us will feel similarly about Spotify - and other similar brands. And what about your innovative idea? Will it be old news next week?

Our lives are built on systems of systems everywhere without being aware of their inner workings. Tax, health, and education systems jump into my mind, but I could have easily said transportation, energy, and communications. Some are fraught with decades of under-investment; others are fully modernised and awash with investment. We may not care how these systems of systems work so long as they do. Thinking in terms of systems helps us frame our problems into comprehensive solutions, building resilience into how they interoperate with other systems. A framework that makes it easier for us to inspire innovation across communities in the pursuit of confidence and assurance that we are growing and being safer. And to facilitate wealth and prosperity for many. But not everyone.

Design for obsolescence

When we think in systems we are playing unwittingly with the trilogy of temptations, weaving more intricacy into our capacity to cope when under stress. Not just the understanding of material resources we need - oil, grain, and data - but also cognitive resources to understand the implications of our decisions - time, space, and people. As MIT's Peter Senge profoundly said, *"businesses and human endeavours are systems...we tend to focus on snapshots of isolated parts of the system. And wonder why our deepest problems never get solved."* [15]

The trilogy of temptations is perfectly amplified through the ease society disposes of electronic gadgetry, whether broken, unfixable or no longer serving a purpose. A by-product of the instant gratification culture that compromises any idea of 'making do with what we have.' A culture that many will criticise the 'industry' for as they seem to arbitrarily decide their product is 'end of life,' forcing customers to 'upgrade' to avoid missing something everyone else has got. A feeling we seem to increasingly dislike but will complain we had no choice if we want to 'keep up.' And when this happens, our perspective switches from mutual gain to mistrust and doubt. When we realise the supplier is treating us as customer attrition fodder, we can be made to feel inconsequential and forgotten.

The business world hangs on to the status quo bias knowing likely we will not 'switch' loyalty, despite anger at price hikes, service disruption and product obsolescence. And we comply because the effort to change and the lure of something promised lets us 'forget.' But when we stop to seriously think and diverge our understanding of the situation we are being placed in by others, we realise we have succumbed to the trilogy of temptations.

The days where we 'made do and mended' have all but disappeared, with most products not designed for repair, or worse still, designed for early obsolescence. When my daughter's iPhone needed a new battery, I thought we could sort this out ourselves without going to a repair shop. I reasoned that it could not be that hard, given it is only the battery to replace after all. But after looking at the 'how to' video on YouTube, I was less confident I could repair it without breaking the phone, and as a result, the kit is still in the drawer. The same drawer that is full of old tech is sitting there until I get around to sending it off to be recycled.

Because my family wants to be more environmentally responsible, I will take some convincing as to whether we need new gadgets in the future. If we do, I would be more mindful to ask about how the gadget is designed for longevity, adaptability, repairability and disassembly using renewable, environmentally, and socially responsible materials. And to be honest, I do not see many that can do that.

Right now, even if I were offered the latest tech gadget for free, I would probably say no.
Debbie Ward, Director, Cirklo Consult

Free Guy understood DBOFO. He was comfortable with all of the stages of our deal, right until the Outcome stage, where he could see the disparity and looming disappointment. He was less interested in the actual cost (partially true, of course) but more focused on weaponising his people with the tools to create the growth he knew his company needed. The deal was not about technology but countering the exuberance of something new.

When ethics meet silicon

Soon that car in front of you will be not driven by a fellow human being but by a computer built of million lines of software code. Up to now the design of a modern car has been a highly optimised piece of engineering, increasingly reliant on powerful technology assets - synthesised to work in complete digital and physical harmony. Some will call this a digital twin entirely represented in the physical and digital form to assist in the design, fault diagnosis and performance optimisation. To the car owner, an effortless experience is secured and focused entirely on them - and their expectations of value. In DBOFO terms it *'does what it says on the tin.'*

But the landscape is changing, and no longer can these tightly coupled assets exist in a bubble of engineering excellence and persuasive marketing. What was once a complicated engineering problem is now shifting into a more complex ethical problem space with the advent of self-driving autonomous vehicles. Now our desire for experience has upped the ante to figuring out how to get a car's computer to behave like us.

A system of systems problem, questioning how we delegate a digital brain to drive a vehicle and the ramifications for ethics, law and onwards. We will expect these self-driving algorithms to figure out what our brains did before - but safer. Now we have to programme the car's brain to ask; swerve to avoid the parents with the pram who just stepped right out in front of me or mount the pavement knocking down the elderly pedestrian? Or steer right to avoid hitting fellow human beings at any cost and run into the lamppost instead, injuring the driver in the process? This a problem that science alone cannot answer, requiring a much wider debate around the liability and tolerance of society to adopt such a change. Who will be liable when an AI fails or malfunctions, who decides what is a failure versus malfunction and how opaque is human decision-making in all of this? Human outcomes are the only things that matter, and when we think about technology's contribution, it is those that start with the O and work back that will thrive.

The missing signature

Back to Free Guy. His mindset that day was about acknowledging the change his business was about to embark on. He was accountable, and through his colleagues had started the entire process that led to the meeting that day. He had budget and commitment to go ahead, so all it needed was his red pen to sign it off. In sales parlance, the deal was 'hot to trot,' 'good to go' and 'in the can.' I nearly said a certainty but who says that?

This was not a casual drive-by chat about the formidable power of geeky software. On the contrary, it was a serious commercial procurement exercise that, as you may reflect from your own experiences, comes with the most granular tick-box governance and excruciating pain for the bid teams involved. But for our team, we had got to the pinnacle and had been selected as the winner, or so we thought until Free Guy pulled out his red pen, crossed out the numbers and said, *'even if this was free I wouldn't sign.'*

Free Guy knew he had to raise the game of his people competing in an ever-changing construction design and engineering industry. An industry which attracts attention from significant political, social, and environmental forces. An industry still enormously proud of its traditions in pencil, paper, and computer-aided drawings despite being surrounded by calls for massive digital change. An industry near the bottom of digital maturity league tables, with Victorian-style supply chain disciplines. Soon entry to bidding for new work would only go to those businesses embracing digital platforms and methods. For this reason, eyes were on Free Guy to make the right call. But for us, he was making the wrong call by not signing our deal!

je n'ai pas de regrets

Have you ever regretted a purchase you wished you had not committed to? Gym memberships, football transfers and DIY extensions are top of mind no doubt. Or more short term the over-eating at a restaurant buffet to *'get my money's worth'* or trying to break a losing streak at the roulette table. Either way, I am sure you will argue your decision was a stroke of genius and that any day now your vision will be proclaimed a success. I am describing something known as the fallacy of sunken cost. A situation when we over-commit to something we have not taken advantage of sufficiently whilst still spending money to avoid the head-hanging admission of failure. [16] A horrible feeling that we know deep down that we will never get our money's worth from our efforts. And all because we cannot bring ourselves to say, *'I got it wrong.'*

Is it stress related? Studies have shown that 'abnormal evaluation of costs and benefits' is a real thing induced by chronic stress levels with which we might not identify.[17] Put bluntly in our attempt to be more successful, with technology as our partner in crime, are we lowering the quality of the decisions we make? Or is the other way round? Are we better at making value judgements on the technology we need and becoming more assured that we are meeting stated outcomes? We will all have arguments for and against here.

Writing on the wall

Steve Ballmer, the then Microsoft CEO, called it *"hogwash"*. He was referring to a Harvard Business Review post that suggested that technology was fast becoming commoditised, embedded, invisible and no longer mattered.[18] The article's author, Nicholas Carr, argued that technology was heading the same way as the railroad, the telegraph, and the car. He asserted that the assumption that *"technology's potency and ubiquity have increased, so too has its strategic value"* was a mistake.

Reading this today we might argue that Carr in 2003 was completely wrong when considering how businesses worldwide have transformed their operations and the lives of so many through technology. Look at how we now, for example, enjoy secure digitised channels to pay for goods and services online in seconds compared to hours and days before. Technology is now so immersed in daily life that it would be hard not to see its strategic value. So Carr was wrong? Perhaps Free Guy might have had sympathy with Carr. He too believed success for his business would be less about choosing the best technology than empowering people to achieve sustainable outcomes and growth. A point of view echoed by Michael. E. Porter, an American economist, and social strategist, *"a company can only outperform its rivals if it can establish a difference that it can preserve."*[19] Preservation of advantage. Isn't this why we do what we do, in business and life generally - preserve our advantage? With or without technology.

In sports, we speak about driving hard to overpower competitors to win the game. In business, we talk similarly about unique selling points and distinct value propositions. And in life, we strive to feel healthier, more educated, and safer to help us and our loved ones to achieve one goal or another. The rise of the robot is the perfect metaphor for how business is tempted to grab the advantage that Porter speaks of.

We, Robot

Remember when you would ring up a customer services helpline and speak to a fellow human who would fix your issue? Now we have humanised interfaces called 'triage bots,' given names we call our pets and children, like Terri and Tobi. These computer gadgets are available 24 hours a day, trained to respond to our most frequent questions. And when they cannot help us, they are programmed to follow business logic rules to pass us up to a human being for resolution. What is there not to like?

Building computers to behave like humans is not new. It is quite a well-trodden path that did not start in Silicon Valley with the characters you might think. Since Alan Turing in the 1950s spoke of whether 'computers can think', entire industries have been racing to 'crack the code'. [20] And if I may indulge slightly to rebalance a distortion of computing history. There is no question Mr Turing and others did pioneer breakthroughs in how to digitise how we consume information. But much of their took influence from a different century, via a young woman called Ada Lovelace.

Ada drafted a paper in the early years of the 19th century outlining a programmable language for scientific machines. Yes, that's right, the 19th century. An insight that lay the foundation for what we take for granted today - including my Spotify <u>innovative thing</u> and perhaps yours too. [21] And one final thing about Mr Turing. Every time I spend endless minutes trying to spot fire hydrants or traffic lights before a website identifies me as a human being, not a robot, I think of him and inwardly smile (groan). You might have met these clever little widgets yourself - known as CAPTCHAS - but may not realise that the T stands for Turing.[22] However, I digress and probably not for the last time!

Tech for good

The natural excitement of getting a computer to do jobs we no longer want to do is compelling and sensitive. And in VUCA times, anything that can remove fragility from our lives is a good thing. Terri and Tobi and their robot family never go on holiday, need payment, nor suffer from hangovers and dodgy stomachs. They do not feel pain or emotion and as such, cannot empathise with our plight when we need someone to open up to. And because we are not digital computers we cannot understand what it must be like to be them. Not yet anyway.

Which explains why the conversation we have with Tobi and Terri is so unhuman and devoid of feeling towards us that it begs the question, *'who is this helping'*? The designers of Tobi and Terri will argue vehemently against my supposition. They will point to their iterative cognitive design process that continually optimises the rat-a-tat flow of the chat box conversation with us. They will also point to the simplification of customer service that speaks directly to our self-centred desire to be agile and innovative - and on our terms.

I love my bank's phone app. At any time, I can pay money in and out and check my balance. This is technology working for me, the customer, doing what any customer wants. But I cannot talk to a person unless I speak to a 'Bot' who does not understand my circumstances or my pain.

Why does my bank think this is Customer Service? It is far away from my first job working in a Foreign Exchange Dealing Room. Every one of us had to spend time on the Customer Query Desk. Every customer call was a VIP call. Our job was to listen, understand, and question for details around the problem and find a solution. Success was met through empathy and understanding the emotions of the person on the other end of the phone having a problem.

I ask why these 'Bots' are seen as an alternative to real people. Complicated problems need understanding, friendliness, and empathy from human beings.
Belinda Rushton, Account Director, Ricoh UK Limited

But what if these bots are not designed to help us but their owners instead? What if Terri and Tobi are outward symbols of how these businesses believe they can preserve their advantage? And not to our advantage. And isn't this our fault anyway because of our desire to get to places faster? Who wanted a customer service desk that 'went home'? And hold music? Agh! So 1980s.

This is not a new phenomenon, of course. The use of automation can be traced back to the early 19th century when looms were programmable using pre-punched cards to accelerate the textile industry. A foundation stone for worker opposition (Luddites) to new technology still is prevalent today.[23] And if the bot is the metaphor for winners then we can only applaud the innovation and creativity of their designers. Pressing home advantage is something we are bought up on - in education, in work, in life generally - so for these businesses a bot is a useful tool. The bot helps their owners redistribute human effort into more qualitative activities, making their business more predictable and profitable whilst giving us, their customers, better outcomes. The bot exists because they represent progress and as we know for anyone to outperform rivals they must *establish a difference that they can preserve.'* Do you agree?

As a side note, the first bot, ELIZA, was created in 1966. So to take half a century to mature this particular innovation is not too unreasonable unless you consider them to still be a 'work in progress' or the Devil's own work. [24]

Hint

Go back to the innovative idea I spoke about at the start of the book. Think about how your experience of the innovative thing makes you feel - happy, positive, productive, or otherwise. Now scribble down on your pad, whiteboard or in your head each of the DBOFO labels - design, build, operate, function, and outcome. Under each heading, consider your feelings when you think of your chosen innovation. You may be 'pleased' with the <u>design</u> but 'frustrated' with its <u>operation</u> under a specific condition where you want it to work for you. The <u>build</u> of the product may fit your lifestyle and other innovations you use. Or you felt happy (or sad) with the <u>outcome</u> when under pressure to get a result. I am intrigued to see if you find it easier to consider words under the outcome label but harder for the others. Maybe this is because you only really care about the experience and know that there are alternatives you can always try. And to balance your investigation, try a less satisfactory experience. Why did the outcome never turn out as you thought?

━━━

Why did I ask you to do this? Free Guy was unconsciously taking the DBOFO challenge and telling us he could not see success. In his mind, the O for Outcome was missing despite the promise of innovation and transformation from our side of the table. How often do we pay for something cool and innovative only to realise the outcome was not going to meet our desirable, feasible and viable needs? Remember the fallacy of sunken cost. And even when something is free, do we unconsciously forego an outcome because *'after all, it was free'* so it isn't costing us anything anyway?

The next chapter will explore why we put faith in what we can see and what others tell us to be so. A place where culture, leadership, and rules encourage us to have the confidence that we are right.

CHAPTER 2

SEDUCED BY CONFIDENCE

"The brain is a machine for jumping to conclusions."
– DANIEL KAHNEMAN

When bosses at a Soviet Union factory set quotas on nail production by quantity, workers diligently churned out thousands of small nails. Unfortunately, their customers wanted the nails to hang heavy chandeliers. Soon houses echoed the sound of chandeliers crashing to the floor. When the bosses realised this, they set the quota by weight, so the factory produced bigger nails that weighed a pound each. Had they made useless nails to improve their metrics and not with an outcome for their customer in mind? [25]

The nail story might be a fable, but we may all point to stories where the obsession with the 'number' obscured reason and logic.

The finite game

There is only one game in town, where the rules and players are known, and the outcome is absolute, win or lose. A finite game that is understood by all those taking part - players and spectators alike. A game of quarters, halves, and year ends, where pipelines, forecasts and budgets are tactical chatter. A game where anything that threatens the outcome is removed from the field of play.

But there is another game being played at the same time - the infinite game. A game where rules and players change, players are not known to each other and where even the game changes.[26]

In business, the infinite game is quite different. In the infinite game, the goal is not to win - but to keep playing. A messy, unpredictable, and exceptionally complex game often at odds with those who strive for certainty and predictability. Players come at the game from all angles, often in complete conflict with a perception of outcome and success - with many oblivious to each other's strengths and weaknesses. It was James Carse, a religious scholar, who in 1986 wrote about this very real aspect of our lives suggesting *"Finite players play within boundaries; infinite players play with boundaries."* [27] Subtle but significantly different.

Nuclear armament, for example, could never be called a finite game. If someone thinks they have won - by pressing the button - we all tragically lose. But we now seem to make everything a game that can be won. Consider how climate change is encapsulated into consumable metrics - offset targets, carbon emissions and forecast models - that suggest progress toward measurable goals. The finite game of winning and losing is the territory of our Converger self. Once someone says there is a game to be won we kick into action and take up the challenge. Like when a ball appears, and jumpers are put down as goal posts. Game on.

Compensation matters

In 1911 when Frederick Taylor introduced the theory of scientific management, the pursuit of certainty in business was born.[28] Taylor argued that business managers would never have the control they desperately needed without a scientific approach to controlling production and output. Like a football coach looking to drive out performance dips and loss of form, business managers would increasingly use technology to drive out inefficiency and uncertainty in systems and processes. This naturally led to the need to measure, monitor and identify areas for operational efficiency.

The certainty of zeros and ones

Beyonce might have sung, *'put a ring on it,'* but the business world may be singing loudly, *'put a number on it.'* Numbers dominate our lives. We seem to be on a mission to codify everything into a number that we can track and justify in one way or other. Take the well-known consumer satisfaction measurement - the Nett Promoter Score (NPS). Based on a single question - *'how likely you are to recommend our business'* - against a scale of 0 to 10, NPS is a building block for many industries today; used to assess consumer sentiment and measurement of contractual compliance.

I worked for a time in the facility management sector and recall the near obsession with the NPS scorecard. Driven by contractual rules, these providers would turn to technology increasingly to help predict service outcomes against the NPS. It was a significant aspect of the business model and was where an advantage could be won or lost. On one hand, there is nothing negative here but at times the over-indulgence in technology as the answer left many scenarios inadequately understood and overly complicated through the technology deployed. Those smiley face machines in airports and retail parks are all part of the strategy to 'collect data' to support the certainty game.

But sometimes these schemes would backfire. Flight attendants at United Airlines express real-time thoughts of management performance using a scoring mechanism called -the FPS - Flight Attendant Promoter Score. [29] A controversial scheme born from a crew scheduling conflict that tries to mix human emotion with a numerical scorecard. Such examples are everywhere and in fairness represent an attempt to quantify a situation. But do they ever help positively and is the human always the worse off?

When we mix absolute measurements and benchmarks, with the variable of human emotions and feelings, things get messy. And despite trying to categorise and label human behaviour into convenient buckets, there is always the threat of complexity throwing a few curve balls at us -

no matter how smart we thought we had been.

In walks complexity

A communication signal covers the planet, yet only half the world's population is online. [30] Of course, people will choose to be offline, but many more are excluded for a whole host of factors, i.e., money, skills, access, support systems and culture. This human exclusion is staggering when you think of the number of unused devices we might have in our households or businesses. [31]

But this is the problem right here. Decision makers will be urged to find a way to quantify a known problem like digital exclusion. And when they identify a gap between current and desired state outcomes they go 'hell for leather' to close the said gap. It becomes a programmatical task to fund activity to do so. And whilst this is not wrong nor to be underestimated in any shape or form, it is only when diverging our thinking that we see the game is not exclusively finite, but infinite too.

Our Diverger self will realise there are shades of digital exclusion that are wickedly complex and do not easily conform to columns in spreadsheets and material delivery of resources. How can they? Somewhere between the absolute numbers, hard-coded policies, and belief systems, lie the frailties of each of us as we try to understand the problem better. Digital exclusion like many other wicked societal problems is a complicated conversation, especially when that conversation is also a complex one and our thinking is centred on the former, and not the latter.

A 17-year-old care leaver received a device and a router as part of a support package. This very quickly became an important source of support and advice for her. Now she was able to access what she needed at whatever time of day she needed it, finding forums and groups of other youngsters with similar needs to her own.

Unfortunately, the router broke, and she was concerned that she would be held responsible. It transpired that it was not broken at all but merely had run out of data for that month. No one had told her this would happen, so as a result, she had lost her lifeline to her network. Better informed, she was back online straight away.

This relates to the notion of neo-liberalism that can be misguided if not thought through deeply enough.
Paul Finnis, CEO, Digital Poverty Alliance

It is easy to see technology as a coach, mentor and advisor, codifying everything known to make it easier for us to digest, reason and make decisions. A situation that works well when we know that the problem we face will respond well to the linear approach to resolution i.e., a decision to lose two kilograms in weight in the next six months. But not acceptable when the issue is messy and unpredictable, complex and full of unknowns i.e., medical conditions and financial liquidity.

We have the answer, but what was the question?

Hundreds of people were gathered in a vast ballroom in a Madrid hotel. The CEO had just laid out the purpose of the next three days, articulating that the sales number was not big enough. Instead of X, it was Y, so the instruction to the group was to find Z. I sat in awe, like the kid in the sweet shop, surrounded by the brightest brains in our company. The CEOs' exam question asked us to consider our top clients, reflect on their problems and plans, and find ideas that would help them achieve more. I will never forget the energy in the room that day. It was a veritable factory of cognitive power and intensity.

My group looked at a large telecommunications provider. We all stood up, firing ideas and counter thoughts onto big sheets on the wall, sharing perspectives on the customers' problems and which of our solutions fitted best. The entire room - football pitch size - was doing the same for their respective customer. However, I was troubled, and eventually, my curiosity got the better of me. I asked, *"now we have momentum, why not call up the customer right now to get their feedback on whether we are hot or cold?"* I rationalised that the customer would be pleased to know we were thinking of them in such a way.

I can still see the amusement on the faces of my colleagues. One told me, *"Paul, this is not how we do it. We find the ideas to go into the pipeline number the CEO wants, and then we go and speak to the customer when we have the green light to go ahead."* I countered, *"but surely if all we are doing is speculating about coming up with the number for the CEO, aren't we going to find that when we speak to the customer, we might be wrong?"*

Three days later the missing value (Z) had been found and

congratulations echoed around the ballroom in a fanfare of teamwork, creativity, and purpose. The finite game had been won that day. On the flight home, I went through my experiences and tried to see both sides of the fence. If I were the customer, someone we had decades of doing business with, I would feel we had missed a fantastic opportunity to build more vital trust by sharing our ideas right away. But then, from the CEO's shoes, this annual event had been heralded as a successful cog in the wheel of sales optimisation. It was part of the DNA, and for some, it was folklore.

Seduced by numbers

The CEO had a complicated yet not unique problem to solve - a lack of a qualified sales pipeline. She was heading down a tried and tested path to resolution by bringing all her people together to find the missing number. But I also felt she might be having an internal dilemma too. Her customers were shifting from just playing the finite win at all costs game to a more purpose-driven infinite strategy, where diverse thinking featured higher up in their plans. Had the CEO got a sales team with muscle memory for only playing the game a certain way and being unable to shift gears? A group of Convergers aligned to compensation, certainty in finding numbers and hitting deadlines, but not supported to explore their Diverger's curiosity streak. Was her confidence misjudged when it came down to how dependable her 'missing number' actually was?

Goodhart's Law states, *"when a measure becomes a target, it ceases to become a good measure"* [32]. A statement that could easily describe businesses and governments everywhere through their presentation of absolute numbers to their audiences. Think back to how media and politicians threw around the 'R number' to focus citizen attention on the rise and fall of the 2020 pandemic. [33] Did we substitute the reality of our situation because of the way 'the number' was presented to us in such an absolute fashion? Were the numbers sufficient to anchor our own stories to what was on the screens? Or did the numbers reassure us and stifle panic in the streets?

Who are we talking about

In finite games, It is a common tactic to invest heavily in understanding the other teams on the pitch - customers and competitors. A tactic that is increasingly reliant on technology to drill down into the most granular slice and dice of demographics, searching for golden nuggets to justify product development investment, sales campaigns, or acquisition strategy. A tactic that might be the difference between preserving an advantage over a competitor or falling behind. An exercise aided by unlimited amounts of bigger and bigger datasets, helping to target and message potential buyers with even more accuracy than before.

Despite having all the technology at our fingertips to run and track marketing campaigns, all we learned was that people no longer wanted what we were offering. We were witnessing an astonishing collapse in our response rates. Each month the downloads of our whitepapers declined until they hit zero, and we watched LinkedIn messenger overtake people's willingness to accept phone calls. At first, we tried to solve the problem by broadcasting louder using the same message on different channels. That failed too. I know now that we had a people problem.

We had been dehumanising them, calling them 'prospects,' treating them as groups and converging too much on the data. We had lost sight of something important: a social revolution had been going on whilst we were not looking. We stopped converging on numbers, changed tack, and returned to seeing people like people again. We launched communities so we could share knowledge collaboratively and without hierarchy. We established Advisory Boards and filled them with current and future clients, industry magnets who understood how to be genuine on social media, and executive coaches who helped us make it personal. Curious people who challenged our thinking.

It was a fast and healthy way to reframe our offering, allowing us to get back on track. We solved our challenges by becoming better listeners and celebrating our inbuilt virtues of curiosity and empathy. Technology and data still played a big part, but the balance had been reset to a more equal and healthy partnership with humans.
Catherine Coale, Freelance Marketing Strategist

The theory goes that once we know what people want we can design a viable and desirable solution. It is why we have cookies on our machines and explains why Mr Zuckerberg's said, *"we run ads."* Tactics that we now take for granted when we run out onto the finite game pitches, where we know there is only one goal in mind - to win. And it is because we are hard-wired to put things into categories.

Called the 'exposure effect,' we have a compulsion to divide ourselves into camps due to our oxytocin hormone that can trust and cooperate with one group whilst being hostile to the other. And it is this categorisation bias, with us since birth, which now encourages us to look to computers to mimic our behaviour to further cement 'them' and 'us.'

The fridge is talking to Alexa

To Hannah Fry, TV presenter and mathematician, the news left her dumbfounded and led her to exclaim, *"I just do not know what on Earth that means."* [34] This was Fry's reply to the news that soon, there will be fridges boasting 'Artificial Intelligence (AI) Ready' labels. The mind boggles with implications for our domestic arrangements. Will the fridge and the kettle collaborate to ensure a steady supply of milk and water for our cuppa? Will the refrigerator be friends with Alexa sharing our innermost eating habits to optimise shopping deliveries? And if this use of AI helps us become healthier citizens living longer, what is the problem?

The technology industry is built on experimentation and prototyping of early ideas and prototypes, seeking development partners and investors to get behind their vision to find the next big thing. A frenzy of investment would entice early adopters to come on board, build momentum and convince others to follow suit. The queues outside Apple stores for the latest and greatest are a visible sign of such early adoption at work, and the annual tech fests in Las Vegas are another.

I am talking about <u>Solutionism</u>. A characteristic labelled as *"an intellectual pathology"* by Evgeny Morozov, limits how we solve problems based on our ability to understand what is happening. [35] It is why designers and software developers will go to extraordinary lengths to demystify complicated issues into neat lines of code, packaging up what they hope to be the next 'big thing.' And solutionists are everywhere defined in my mind as people with great ideas eager to solve problems. Except at times, the problems they see are NOT the problems that matter the most.

My exposure to solutionism was during the Internet of Things (IoT) explosion, a time highlighted by the ability to take cheap microelectronic sensors and connect software to business processes to produce previously hidden insight. And at a scale unimaginable just a few years earlier. People would call it a paradigm shift, presumably to resonate with shock and awe in the listening audience. A shift that opened Pandora's box of everyday use cases that were identified as annoying, inefficient, and prime to be 'IoTified.' And no better place to highlight this amazing technology was the ability to monitor washroom occupancy. Yes, I am going to talk about toilets.

Who is listening

The concept was that if no one has been inside a washroom since the last cleaning cycle, then there was no need to schedule a cleaner visit. Made a lot of sense but how could they achieve this when in large city skyscrapers the number of toilets would be in the hundreds? Simple. Placing cheap sensors at the entry to the washroom to detect movement across the threshold to the restroom, helped service providers achieve significant productivity gains while still maintaining hygiene standards. Think of those. Except in one case, when it was realised that placing sensors directly above each urinal in the male restroom - with the 'microphone enabled' - produced some interesting graphs of 'noise' activity.

The office was old and designed for a different era." Yeah, it is looking a little tired. I am not sure the space is working for anyone anymore," said my client. It was clear that what the client said was a universal truth across the workforce. They had become a digital-first company and needed spaces to collaborate, take online calls or host events. What they had was an open-plan office with a hotdesking system and a couple of meeting rooms. The client concocted a plan to prove that although desks were being booked, they were not using those spaces. Why? Because staff were using coffee shops, squatting in meeting rooms and doing nothing but being sat at their hot desks.

The client installed sensors over the weekend to collect the data to make their case to HQ. Come Monday, when the staff were back, they noticed a small box under the desk peering at their legs. By the time the morning coffee break came about, the conspiracy was out there. What had gone from a data collection activity had now become a case of enterprise up-skirting scandal. A double whammy for the company facing a people's problem through their attempt to solve another people's problem.

You see, the real issue was less about who sat where and

more about office culture - which cannot be fixed by a technology solution!

Matthew Marson, Co-Founder, Smart Building Bootcamp

And what about when Google's innovation known as Google Glass, ended up being banned by restaurants and cinemas, when it was discovered users could record video discretely, giving rise to the term, *glasshole.*' [36] Solutionism is everywhere.

The architecture industry for example is often vilified for building the equivalent of the 'solution button.' One only has to look around the city landscapes and urban areas to spot examples. When he exclaimed, *"what is proposed is like a monstrous carbuncle on the face of a much loved and elegant friend,"* King Charles III created a veritable storm. [37] He was referring to the proposed extension to the National Gallery in London but had a list of others on the naughty step. He was alluding to the blind-sided nature of the architecture industry to use presumption in place of investigation when presenting their ideas.

I have met many solutionists, and at times I have no doubt been one myself. The one consistent characteristic they all have is absolute confidence that their solution is a nailed-on certainty of being a roaring success. They have an unwavering belief that they understand the problems people face and that their solution holds the key.

Do you remember the popularised motivation when people talked about innovation, *'build a better mousetrap and the world will beat a path to your door'*? A well-used metaphor that entices people to believe everyday problems can always be improved through innovation. This might explain why in America the number of 'mice catching' patents runs to thousands. But technology isn't magic. It's made and programmed by humans who suffer from prejudice and bias at every tap and swipe.

Put the human first

Think again about your innovative thing and the problem it has helped you overcome or the opportunity it has provided to you. As you do I would like you to consider these three questions.

- Was the solution instantly desirable for you or were there hurdles to get across before you knew you wanted it?
- Was the solution viable for you right away? How did you approach affordability, usability, and functionality? How hard was it for you to overcome any barriers before the innovation made its impact?
- Finally, how feasible was it for you to adopt the innovation? Did it work in your world right away or were there conditional factors that took time to mature first?

I have met many solutionists adept at answering these questions fully - on our behalf. They do this through a deep understanding of the problem facing the other person. But I have also met those who pay scant attention to what their solution means to others, preferring to 'assume' that what they are designing will be desirable, viable and feasible for others. They will argue that their wizardry is strengthened by market research that confirms there is a need out there. But as someone once told me, market research means people not saying what they think, and then not doing what they say.

So how can we push back on ourselves, not to artificially challenge what people say to us about good ideas and technology's role, but to contribute open feedback to help ourselves?

Be a cynic for a day

One way to counteract this rush to solutionism is to be a cynic or non-believer. I am talking about when someone tells us something they believe is good for us, but we just don't believe them. A cynic can be seen as destructive and suspicious and we probably all know a cynic in our lives - and at times we have played the role too. When a cynic meets a solutionist the dynamics can be explosive and inspirational (like in Dragons Den). The cynic can be just what a budding solutionist needs by challenging their self-interest in their big idea and questioning the underlying motive. And the value of the cynic in a solutionist and finite world is to be the voice of diversity, not obstruction. Someone to say, 'this is a bad idea' and stimulate deeper thinking as to what might be missing.

So imagine you are part of a business decision to solve a problem, where evidence and confidence are mounting, convincing you and others that you are on the right track.

We all like to think we are all on the 'same bus,' don't we? You have done your legwork, built a prototype and gained positive early adopter feedback. But before you press ahead you do something different and run a <u>cynic clinic</u>.

Hint

Produce a brief synopsis of the problem statement and the proposed solution on which you are working. You might have a prototype to share as well. Then invite people outside your problem space - a peer on the management team, a team colleague, or an independent coach. Share the synopsis or prototype with them at the start of the session. Ask them to read or experience your idea in <u>total silence</u>. This is key because you want them all to receive the idea precisely at the same time without any influence from opinionated chatter. Then you ask them to find holes in your thinking by asking them to play the role of the cynic. Help them by asking them to consider the desirability, viability, and feasibility of your idea. Just let them speak and listen to what they have to say. Allow ten minutes and see what you have learned. Try and avoid negotiating on the solution; just soak up the feedback and put it to good use when you think about your problem statement.

The Cynic Clinic is a tactic to push you out of your converged comfort zone. A place we all find ourselves in when working on a new idea and where those around us comply with the groupthink prevalent. It is a courageous thing to do but in a world of uncertainty and crisis of prioritisation, it might be a tactic that will reap benefits further down the line. Another tool to pop into the Diverger's toolkit.

It's a kind of magic

Created by Gartner, respected market research analysts, the Magic Quadrant™ (MQ), has been a source of evidence for technological solutions to businesses' problems - similar to the Which? magazine has been for consumer products. The MQ gives a glance at which technology companies are seen as challengers, leaders, niche players and visionaries, helping inform investors and commentators on which companies held an advantage over their peers. [38] I can testify that being able to stand in front of a prospective customer knowing your proposition was on 'the MQ' was often a deal-breaker moment. And for the customer hoping to gain comfort in such analysis, It was not a lot different from the Ancient Greeks standing in front of the Oracle asking whether their journey would be a successful one or not.

Hyped up

And like anything magic, the thrill of mystery and suspense isn't far away, which may explain the other initiative run by Gartner, known as the Hype Cycle™.[39] Each year they produce varying reports that again share insight for investors, customers, and suppliers about the maturity, adoption, and application of specific technology genres i.e., drones for shopping drop-off, AI-controlled cars and social media cha- trooms valued as non-fungible tokens. Or in fact, none of these things transpired and was just hype.

Technology hype is visualised as a helter-skelter journey from the predicted <u>trigger for innovation</u>, then up to a <u>peak of inflated expectations</u>, down into a <u>trough of disillusionment</u>, back up to a <u>slope of enlightenment</u> until finally <u>plateauing</u> into mainstream acceptance and resilience. Phew! Who doesn't want to be on the slope of enlightenment? Who doesn't want innovation that will take them across the slopes and plateaus while avoiding troughs? This language is a seduction that obfuscates the blind spots from view. And the crazy thing is that we know it is. So why do we do it? Because it breeds confidence and for investors, this is what they need to see. And when we are tuned into believing what we see we will unconsciously shut down our ability to see what we can't.

Hidden from plain sight

During World War Two, the United States Air Force engineers faced the problem of why they were losing crews and planes to enemy fire during combat missions. From bullet hole data they concluded adding extra armour to the plane's fuselage would improve the chances of a safer return from battle. A logical solution from the data they had available. But then in stepped Abraham Wald. A bit of background on Wald. First of all, Wald was not American - he was Hungarian. Second, he had escaped Nazi persecution. It is most likely, therefore, that his experiences and perspectives were vastly different from his colleagues that day.

Wald disagreed with his colleague's assessment of the problem. He argued that the armour should not go where the bullet holes were but should go where the bullet holes were not - the engines. The question Wald was asking that no one else was, where are the missing bullet holes? Wald rationalised that those surviving bombers rarely had damage in the engine because they would not have returned to base if they did. He convinced them to look at the bullet hole data differently and to look for analysis they could not see. With the new analysis, engineers reinforced the bombers' engines and more crews survived combat. Wald was a voice of diversity in that room and lives were saved because of it. [40]

This example speaks of our tendency to look at the information visible to us, support our decisions, and dismiss what is invisible as irrelevant. This is known as survivorship bias and whether we like it or not, it is a bias we use every day without realising it.

I remember vividly visiting my Grandad, the first psychiatrist in Uganda, and exploring anything to do with the workings of the human brain with him. It was this experience that started my journey to be curious about how technology helped humans. In adult life, this curiosity eventually saw me sitting in front of the owners of the JustGiving organisation.

Their business was elegantly simple. They provide a platform to allow people to raise money for worthwhile causes using the power of the internet to make the process as seamless as possible. The journey here was that there was value in the data, but the owners had not found it. On one occasion, we wanted to understand how to maximise donations on the fundraising page. We believe that everything that a donor sees on this page influences their final donation amount. This is an example of where things can go wrong if you do not have a greater understanding of context. The data would suggest you should always show a picture of a bicycle to influence bigger donations. Further analysis shows that this is the algorithm making a suggestion based on what it can see. It transpires that those middle-aged white men who cycle raise more than the average person. Without context, the system thinks it is because of the image of the bicycle.

Business leaders want data to help them tell stories, but often, the data becomes the story itself, and this is entirely wrong. I continue my journey of curiosity, helping others figure out their story first without letting the data take over too soon.

Mike Bugembe, Co-Founder & CEO, Decidable

Premature enumeration

And it gets worse. When we look at the information we have collated to suit our situation we can be trapped in something called <u>premature enumeration</u>. [41] A bias which points to our tendency to slice and dice numbers using ratios, variances, and algorithms before we fully understand what they mean.

I have a Fitbit device that tracks my footsteps. I have a figure in my head of 10,000 steps a day that convinces me that if I hit that number every day, I am doing something good for my health. I will admonish myself when I do not get close to the number and applaud myself when I bust it wide open. I play a game of averages all the time relying on this dumb piece of technology around my wrist. And all the time, I ask myself why I could be so quickly drawn into believing what I see on the screen as a sign of assurance of a healthy lifestyle.

And as we search for evidence to convince us that our decisions are sound we clamour to 'go big' as a form of guarantee that our decisions are sound and robust.

Go large?

Thinking small has been a tactic criticised by many who suggest we jump to conclusions without compiling enough evidence. But thanks to technology such criticism is unfounded with the maturity of Big Data analysis as a tool of discovery and certainty. And in fairness, we are doing a good job. The Genomics study of DNA, predictive maintenance of aircraft engines and weather pattern analysis are lifesaving use cases we now just take for granted. Data science is now an established career path, not just in academia and research but in mainstream business life also. We can now see the clear correlation between cause and effect within the huge data vaults we are collecting, confident that answers to questions we haven't asked yet are in there somewhere. As put by Atul Butte at Stanford, *"hiding within those mounds of data is the knowledge that could change the life of a patient or change the world."* [42] And that is the good side of going big but what are we missing along the way?

Ethnographer, Tricia Wang, reached an exciting observation about mobile phones. She concluded that low-income consumers were ready to pay more for their smartphones. A revelation that Nokia summarily dismissed, because Wang's sample was too small compared to their big data analysis. Wang disagreed, believing her sample was sufficient for Nokia to pivot from making expensive smartphones for the elite to building affordable smartphones for low-income users. Nokia was adamant and dismissed Wang's findings because they could not see them in their 'bigger' datasets. As Wang commented, *"they did not know how to handle data that was not easily measurable and did not show up in existing reports."* [43]

The history of Nokia is well documented, as soon after, it fell off the grid as a serious smartphone player unable to compete with Blackberry and Apple. It could well be that their over-reliance on the 'big' deflected their attention from the 'small,' just when it could have made all the difference. Are we that susceptible to believing that the only way to grow relies on going big? Can we benefit from a different view?

A footnote

The aftermath of the Madrid conference saw my colleagues and I go back to the telecommunications customer with the ideas we had generated. And things were not smooth sailing. First, we did not have the same team available with the passion and vigour from the conference. Second, we

61

had failed to work on our ideas believing what we had would be good enough to inspire our customers. And finally, and most tellingly, we had missed our window of opportunity. The customer hadn't been sitting around waiting for us to turn up. Why would they? We hadn't involved them in our ideas fest. And consequently, they had priorities shifting that negated some of our thinking from Madrid. I reflect that the room that day was too converged on the 'number,' and not on the 'customer,' as we searched for certainty that our sales pipeline was big enough. We should have made that phone call!

We are subjected to a bombardment of information that convinces us we are doing the right thing. Put two people in a room and the chance of this happening is quite likely. And as we get stuck into the conversation we suffer from intellectual arrogance, a characteristic that tends to blind an otherwise intelligent person from recognising the truth. You might read this and feel in your environment you have sufficient checkpoints or habits to prevent this from happening to you and those around you. I say this because it is relevant to the next leg of the trilogy of temptations - innovation. But before you turn the page just take a moment to reflect on your innovative thing and ask why it makes you feel confident.

CHAPTER 3

INNOVATE OR DIE

"Innovation is taking two things that exist and putting them together in a new way."
- TOM FRESTON

Right now I am sitting at *///assist.robot.words.* With just this information it would be possible for you to find me. No need to know my postal address, the city I live near, or even the country where I reside. No, I have not gone mad. These weird-sounding names result from an innovation that carves the earth into three-metre digital squares - fifty-seven trillion of them. A global addressing system called What3words™ assigns each square a unique combination of three random words. This means people can find you without any other information, provided your phone can be traced to that location. [44] You might argue that this example might well be innovative compared to other ways of finding people but not particularly life changing. But as we know, context is everything.

Take the hiker lost on the island of Harris, northwest of the Scottish mainland. The young man was disorientated, with little chance of directing rescue teams to his location. Luckily, he had his mobile phone and an active internet signal. The rescue services asked him to download the What3Words app, and within minutes they had pinpointed his position and, shortly after, delivered him safely by helicopter to the hospital.[45] Now innovation becomes a lifesaver and a case of 'right tech, right place.'

But we are guilty of overusing the innovation word? Do we overindulge the true benefit because it suits our confidence and ego that we are right? Do we in turn dismiss a whole host of factors and contradictory voices that point to our ideas not being as robust as thought? After all, if you can still buy paper maps, and vinyl records and still watch programmes on a black-and-white TV there is a lot of robust resistance to innovation out there.[46]

Take a moment

Think back to the <u>innovative thing</u> that I asked you about earlier. Ask yourself when it works the best - and the least. I am talking about the environment you are in when you get the best experience. What prerequisites need to be in place for it to mean something important to you? The What3Words app might have been innovative that day in the highlands of Scotland, but if the young man had fallen over on a busy Oxford Street in London, the technology would have been down the list. Context is everything. In my humble opinion, a pint of Guinness in a Dublin bar tastes better than consumed anywhere else in the world. Why? Not because the Guinness itself is different, but because it's consumed in Dublin.

The problem with innovation

The mere mention of the word romanticises our view that something incredible is about to happen. But as we are learning with the plethora of smart gadgets for the home, an attractive design does not always become sticky enough for us to influence how we live. Alexa, are you listening? (Of course, you are).

It is one thing to have a ground-breaking idea you believe people want, and another to deliver the resilient outcomes they need. And the reason it is so hard is that it is disruptive, and contrary to what we all think, we are creatures of habit, shying away from disruption and preferring harmony. We might think we need change, but when someone produces a product they believe will help us, it is not always clear whether we will behave as they anticipate.

It is hard

Microsoft had a shout at owning the portable media player market with their Zune™ product. But they fell short of Apple's iPod™. Why? According to Robbie Bach, a former Microsoft executive, *"We just weren't brave enough, honestly, and we ended up chasing Apple with a product that wasn't a bad product, but it was still a chasing product, and there wasn't a reason for somebody to say, oh, I have to go out and get that thing."* [47] I wonder how many innovations go the same way. Not because it lacked the qualities of a strong contender in its market, but because it lacked something else. And something else requires so much more than clever ideas and patents, enthusiastic early adopters and supportive media attention. No, to make an innovation stick, involves an acceptance of two competing philosophies that need to come together to have any chance of success. One is all about design, and the other is all about systems. The combination of these two philosophies means we have to not just *"think like a system, but act like an entrepreneur"* as described fittingly by Matthew Taylor of the Royal Society of Arts. [48]

We may well have great innovative ideas that others support, but when placed inside the 'system' where it needs to function, then the wheels come off. You can't have one without the other. The rise and fall and rise again of the e-scooter spring to mind; of course, now a thing in towns and cities.

Think back to your innovative thing and consider how it merges with a 'system' i.e., e-scooters using the internet and smartphones - that enables you to maximise your enjoyment. Was that always the case or did you have to wait for other components to catch up to realise the full benefit? Did your circumstances change enabling you to acquire the innovation much easier? Did you have to customise the 'thing' to make it work for you?

It turns out that the most successful innovations are of the *'why didn't I think of that'* type. Innovation refers to the development of new ideas or the improvement of existing ideas. And within innovation, there is a spectrum of ideas that covers 'efficiency' through to the 'wicked.' Now I don't have any data on this, but I will guess that the majority of innovations that help us each day are the 'efficiency' type. This makes me look around the room I am in typing these words and can see LED lightbulbs, a left-handed mouse and a bookmark. And when I go into the garage (where the printer lives) I will see that invaluable can of WD40, duct tape and the long-handled hedge trimmer!

But for all of these efficiency innovative ideas to make it to paperclip status, some nuances are more to do with culture, ecosystems, and trust, rather than bits, bytes, and flashing lights.

Is the culture, right?

I have never met a business leader who has not at some point lamented the lack of innovative thinking in their world. They complain that despite believing they have the right culture for open innovation, enthusiasm all but fizzles out after a promising start. To avoid this scenario, leaders will reach out to external consultants, handpicked creative groups, or bank their money on the 'annual' think fest. They do all this not because they can guarantee it will work - who could - but because all they hope for is just one spark of innovation to be effective. Their 'business muscle memory' tells them that this approach has always bought them success. And I share this theory because deep down we all rely on the bias of familiarity. But then I always have in the back of my mind the wonderful short tale from Spencer Johnson, called *'Who Moved My Cheese.'* [49] A book that acts as a nagging reminder that 'our cheese does in fact move' and we should be prepared to go looking for it.

Our bias to go with what we know will often overpower the

desire to go looking for new ideas. We might acknowledge that 'out there' will be a plethora of ideas that could be 'the one,' but we cannot ring-fence time and money to go and find out with abandon and free spirit. So instead, we compromise and create discrete business units and design partners to meet them in the middle under the auspices of a *'you can go wild but within reason'* directive.

Google was one notable business that extolled this idea of free spirit and blue-sky thinking. Their founders, Larry Page, and Sergey Brin wrote, *"this empowers them to be more creative and innovative. Many of our significant advances have happened in this manner."*[50] Back in the day, staff were openly encouraged to ring-fence part of their working week to go wild and think of ideas no matter how wacky and bizarre they might be. Google became the blueprint for others hoping to find the next Steve Jobs or Bill Gates in their midst. But It seemed that the pressure of the finite game affects even the masters of a free spirit when Google pulled back from this bottom-up approach. [51]

It needs scale

I counter this slightly because I am speaking with a commercial head where any idea can only be judged successful if the business is repeatable and lucrative. But innovation can be singular and satisfy its owner completely. Gardeners spring to mind with makeshift tools that 'are fit for purpose.' But I will focus on the commercial aspect because I suspect my readers are sitting largely in that space.

Have you ever taken an Uber ride? If so, would you consider them to be innovative? Let's examine what they do. They exploit the internet, GPS satellite signal, and smartphones - systems and commodities designed by others. The innovation was their thinking. Uber's co-founders Travis Kalanick and Garret Camp, put themselves in the shoes of a consumer and asked a quite simple question, *'What if you could request a ride from your phone?'*

They realised people wanted a service more on their terms rather than the hail-a-ride taxi experience. Why do I need to lose valuable time standing around with my arm up in the air when I could have stayed in the pub or had another ten minutes at my desk? Or stand in a taxi rank at the airport after a long-haul flight? They figured people wanted to get away from this unpredictability and take more control of their onward journeys.[52] And once they started experimenting with their idea, they realised people also did not like surprises on the fare. A double whammy. But perhaps their most significant innovative discovery was that they could be the tipping point to a scalable marketplace, where supply (drivers) and demand (us) held no bounds. Uber's real innovation was its ability to identify a platform that has now spawned other new services, such as Uber Eats™ (food delivery) and Uber Lime™ (e-scooters).[53]

And they are not alone. Born in the cloud platform services are now the norm - eBay, Airbnb, Boohoo and Upwork - to name a few. But did any of these businesses predict this ecosystem dynamic from the start? Perhaps not, and there was no doubt serendipity and luck were factors, but the one thing they all have in common is that they understand growth through scale. And for more traditional businesses where the legacy load and converged thinking is a real issue, the opportunity to stretch from 'solution thinking' to 'platform thinking' can be incredibly rewarding. Innovation is one thing but building a sustainable growth business needs more than cool ideas. But we know this, right?

In Kenya, a substantial percentage of the population lives hours if not days away from the nearest ATM or does not even have a bank account, unable to safely store, save, borrow, and transact money. Instead, the 'unbanked' would carry cash around, leaving them exposed to theft and house burglaries.

Progress came with what started as a philanthropic initiative designed to widen access to micro-loans in rural and lower-income communities. The progress became the largest revenue-generating stream for Safaricom. Progress that became Africa's largest FinTech, setting the precedence for the art of the possible in growing formal financial inclusion of the unbanked in Africa.

Observing what people used the pilot for, rather than what it was originally designed for, resulted in pivoting the 'micro-loan' solution to the money transfer solution with an unintended set of use cases addressing the most pressing, existential needs of the targeted customer base. M-Pesa, a solution using 'simple technology,' transformed people's lives by providing the unbanked with their first-ever access to financial services.[54] The platform led to a halving of armed house robberies, lifting many out of extreme poverty, opening opportunities for entrepreneurs, and resulting in an unexpected range of social benefits beyond anybody's expectations.

Viktoria Vrbiniak ,MBA, Telco Client Leader, IBM

It needs context

When you get a headache, what do you do? Grin and bear it, or take a painkiller? You will likely take the painkiller because you know your headache will have cleared in a few hours. As a result, painkillers are never far from our reach, lurking in bags, glove compartments and kitchen drawers. We have them to hand because we know one day there is nothing else that will ease the pain. They address the most fundamental of human conditions - the avoidance of pain.

Now consider when you feel a little drained or washed out. In this case, you may consider a dose of Vitamin D to help you get that spring back in your step. Or do you think *'I just need some sunlight, or a juicy orange and I will feel as right as rain'*? To many, taking vitamin supplements is just not enough to earn painkiller status. And when we apply this thought to technology, our business 'drawers' are cluttered with gadgets bought to be painkillers but, despite best intentions, lie there as nice to have vitamins. And when we forget about them or convince ourselves that one day we will use them we enter the world of sunken cost fallacy, illusion, and closed thinking.

Is your <u>innovative thing</u> a painkiller for you or just a nice-to-have vitamin that you have other choices available? Does this change depend on your situation and needs? And did it once start as a nice to have, only to flip to painkiller status because of an event you could never have envisaged? Uber might have easily become a vitamin. Plenty of other people offer similar services, and we have many transportation choices rather than a taxi - metro, bike, bus. But Uber's ecosystem has become a de facto tool for many to get around - a bit like Amazon did for getting stuff we want. Both extensible platforms fit neatly with the economies of scale and bottomless supply and demand characteristics. Will they still be around in five, ten or twenty years? Or is that not the point?

It is slow

How long do you think it takes on average for innovation to come to realisation? Five years? Ten? Twenty? No, Thirty years! [55] And this is the bitter pill that business leaders have to swallow. Especially against a perception of 'spin up in seconds tech' promised to investors and customers as the next big thing. Such excitement reaches a fever pitch only to dissipate as the reality of what is real versus make belief starts to show.

Perhaps this is why people will 'rush' a proof-of-concept idea to avoid sluggishness and delay in the decision-making process. Driven by the thought that early adoption is the holy grail to build momentum for the masses to follow, I have seen mock-up demos become productionised with inevitable disappointing outcomes. I have also seen people try to wrap a sales number around 'still in the oven ideas,' leaving the unsuspecting customer with reliability and performance issues down the line. But hang on. Surely, I am talking in the past tense, and with the arrival of 'agile,' such scary stories are now history. I am not so sure.

Agile is one of the most dangerous words in business today; the metaphor for acceleration and speed. The go-faster stripe of modern business strategy. The common thinking is that if you are not agile, you are slow, and if you are slow, you will die. This notion has become so well established that no one even thinks to question it anymore. I mean who would kick off a conversation by saying *'let's talk about how this new idea will make our business less agile in the coming months.'* It wouldn't make sense because the opposite of agile is to be 'clumsy, dull, ignorant, lazy, slow, sluggish, brittle.'

Fr(agile)

It can be no coincidence that in the English language, the word fragile also contains the letters used to make up the word agile. Interesting, isn't it, especially when you think about the world around us right now?

When something is fragile it is susceptible to stress and indication of a problem. If I touch type on this keyboard, I am likely to be quite agile in my word processing output, but if I increasingly smash down on the keys, eventually, the computer will spit out angrily at me and cease to help me. Similarly, when the financial markets collapsed in 2008 fragile outcomes were experienced for many who thought they were being nimble and ahead of the game with their monetary plans. The earth's climate system is reaching fragile levels whilst many of us believe we lead agile lives. We are surrounded by contradictions of agile on one hand but fragile on the other. And many believe our short-term desire to be more agile is having the reverse effect over the longer term. But who publicly wants to speak about fragile?

This talk of agile and fragile is precisely why the fundamental goal of a business is to be sufficiently <u>anti-fragile</u> to ride with the punches and deliver growth.

Factoring resilience and redundancy into business models is now the norm for business design. Diversification is the word of the day as the business seeks multiple routes to market. And in people management, the concept of succession planning is considered vital to ensure expertise is maintained.

Mindset shift

There was a time when agile was not a word used in technology circles, more likely to be used to describe someone's athleticism than a business's ability to adapt to changing market forces. Before agile became de facto, the approach to technology was very much a 'rip and replace' mindset. A time characterised by long incremental steps that seemed to drag on endlessly, often with disappointing results. People would mandate a 'sweat the asset' approach before any replacement talk was allowed. And they were strangled by the rigours of 'raising change requests' that became a creeping death for budget and expectation of a working outcome.

But when agile became a business term the shackles were off. Now we most definitely could have our cake and eat it. Projects that would have taken years to determine whether they worked were now cut into bite-size slices, operating in fast and flowing schedules. Customers were delighted to see outputs regularly done inside a language of scrums and stand-up huddles. What was there not to like? The emancipation of 'failed projects' was complete, and the future looked rosy. Being agile was the ultimate anti-fragile antidote and technology was the toolset that we all thirsted for. 'Long live agile' was heard around boardrooms.

Stability, please

McKinsey, well-respected management thought leader, even coined the phrase, *"agility rhymes with stability"* strapline, to underline the confidence business people have when they talk about all things agile. [56] And why not? An entire industry had built agile into their storytelling, realising it was the codeword to unlock opportunity with a marketplace desperate to get on the 'bus' speeding down the highway.

Uber might have agreed with McKinsey's stability strapline until sued in 2018 for misclassifying drivers as independent contractors. The ruling stipulated that drivers were employees and therefore protected under employment legislation rights. [57] Was this a prime example of a clash of the fast (Uber's business model) with the slow (employment legislation)? In a VUCA world, innovation can be the best thing since sliced bread one day and then the root of all evil the next. A tenuous landscape that Clayton Christensen, author of the *Innovators Dilemma*, warned about the tens of thousands of new product ideas that business introduces each year, only to see a small number make the cut. [58] I lay a wager that none of these product ideas started with fragility in mind. I go further to suggest the innovators were only thinking about how their idea would make the recipient more agile than they were before.

Wild Ducks

We all come across a Wild Duck at one time or other. Such people are employed to provoke open, innovative thought with colleagues and customers alike. Wild Ducks operate freely without the confines of targets and deliverables but are given a free-roaming role to see what they can come up with. And we need Wild Ducks. I was fortunate to work with many who were leading the charge with incredible technological advancements like the Internet of Things, Artificial Intelligence and 3D printing. But as I met more and more of these characters, some of whom are dear friends, I would find myself asking the question *'just because you can, doesn't mean you should, unless you know why.'* A phrase that I would throw back to the Wild Duck fraternity to see what they thought. And many times I would find myself a lone voice when an onslaught of logic was thrown back at me. It was almost like the why had been figured out already, and they (the innovators) were working backwards to find a solution to fit. A room full of solutionists is a beautiful thing to see if you want high energy, creativity, and lots of innovative chatter, but it can be lonely if you are the only person asking why. Does this ring any bells in your world?

Is it change or growth?

Deep down, we seek ways to improve our situation when we believe we are being innovative - a natural event in our evolution as a species. Sometimes we innovate to fix tactical snags in our way, and other times we reach for innovation to change significant situations. It might be a significant event, like a wedding, moving home, or a minor thing, decorating a room or considering a night out.

And in any conversation about change through innovation, two other words circle like birds of prey - transformation and growth. John Maxwell wrote, *"change is inevitable. Growth is optional,"* and I have never met a business leader that wants to talk about anything other than growth. [59] It might be sales performance, production output or share of a particular market, but the language is always the same. Free Guy knew this. He understood change and transformation but only if there was a good chance of growth in the end. But I have seen so many people, myself included at times, dangerously interchange these three words - change, transformation, and growth - especially when there are solutionists and innovators in the room. And the odd Wild Duck!

Change is seen as a specific event, usually self-contained, aimed at replacing something in existence and where we have a good perspective of our outcome. We know this because we know where we are (called the As-Is state), and we can see where we want to get to (called the To-Be state). And from the perspective of technology, change is expected and planned. The language of change fits nicely into the finite game, adhering to the known players, rules, and outcomes. We will use the phrase *'we are all on the same page'* as a litmus test to ensure there was consensus on a new idea or task to undertake. We utter these words to close down diverse thoughts, objections, and alternatives to force the issue to a conclusion. And we do this because when we embark on a change we try hard to frame the event into finite measurements - budgets, deadlines, and sign-off. I will leave you to reflect on your experiences of change, but I hazard a guess there is a mixed bag of successes, failures, and downright disasters in there. And then there is Transformation, which is more about influencing core beliefs and behaviours to achieve the desired result. An event or programme is not singular in duration, but a long-term iterative series of activities designed to affect the future state. I can change the colours of my living room, but it will take more than a lick of paint to transform the experience for my family. A business can implement a new digital system to change how they service customers, but it will take a shift in service mindset to transform what their customers think, feel, say, and do. I can decide to change my diet, but I will need a concerted habit-forming perspective to achieve a transformation in how I think of myself. If change is inevitable and growth is optional then where does transformation fit? Surely this has to sit in between the other two? Change first, then transform and then grow?

The elephant in the room

We are all comfortable with the old versus the new in our lives. But the fallacy of sunken cost and our failure to consider deeply enough what is desirable, viable and feasible outcomes, can come back to haunt us. What we thought was going to help us grow does the exact opposite. Either we failed to understand the problem we thought we had (likely) or the choices we made were flawed (also likely).

When we see a problem that we need to resolve to get a better result we naturally turn on our innovative tap. And when we do we look for ways to show that the innovation has worked. And at that very point in our thinking cycle, we have a choice. Do we go with what we can see - the immediate problem - or do we look ahead and try and anticipate the *bigger picture*? The former meets expectations of cost and time, and the latter talks about how we see growth and resilience. The former appeals to our 'just get it done' mindset, and the latter might mean doing things differently.

You need to look at the bigger picture

Have we all heard this phrase? Would it inspire you or drive you to distraction? Motivational or condescending? Popular with bosses the words would make you stop and rethink your approach or do the exact opposite and hunker down further. Yes, it is cliché time. What about this one, *'you are too far down into the weeds'*? A phrase aimed to encourage people away from getting into the micro details of an issue? I know many people who would be quite happy in the weeds without ever making any tangible progress. But then *'you are too far up in the clouds'* is the counter to this. And then what about this one, *'We have a burning platform issue?'* Derived from the oil industry a sentence that suggests that change can be created by accepting that the status quo is not survivable. A cliché that speaks to the idea that there is a heroic saviour - a human armed with technology - who will lead you through change.

But is the problem that when we hear these words we unconsciously fall into converging on what is comfortable and not what is sustainable? The former ticks the change box but the latter is most definitely optional.

I was homeless when I was fifteen and faced a multitude of different challenges stemming from the physical and psychological effects of those early years. I am one of a small percentage who made it from the bottom to the top, and as such, I decided to use my time, resources, technology, and funding to enable more people to positively transform their lives.

In early 2019 I formed The Positive Transformation Group, a powerful collaboration of organisations supporting charitable opportunities to positively impact one billion lives. A community supplying the right networks, connections, resources, and opportunities to create brighter, better futures. Everything depends on our ability to make other people's lives better.

I can say that transformation is not an overnight siloed event. We have had difficulties, but the growth I have seen in people has been incredible. This is because we started with a human outcome in mind, which made it easier to build something that was going to be scalable and sustainable.

Dan Brown, Founder, Positive Transformation Group

Where am I heading with this? And what has this got to do with innovation? Fair point. So let's think about how our conversations about change, transformation and growth manifest themselves in a practical sense. And it often starts with the WORKSHOP.

The curse of the workshop

When someone says there is going to be a workshop, our hormones excite believing something different is going to happen. After all, they could have called it a meeting so surely this is going to be creative and fun? The sheer word - workshop - can invoke such feelings in people. It is as if the sheer idea we are coming together to 'innovate' is all we need to achieve 'innovation.'

But a workshop needs to leave an impression and not two hours in our calendars every few months. Too often a workshop becomes just a distant memory of a time when everyone was excited and engaged, only to be dismissed when the converged world of business-as-usual kicks in. As David Schonthal, from the IDEO company, puts it, *"I cannot think of many organisations that create a noticeably clear project objective for reflection….usually it is 'Go, go, go, go, go! What is the next step?"*

So let me ask you, what is the purpose of a workshop? To be the best minds together to do something transformational, to address a problem and explore ideas or to review the future and create plans and budgets? All of these and many more I suspect.

Convergers love a 'good workshop.' It is their chance to make progress and to help shape a solution. But a room full of people with the same outlook and mindset might be counterproductive. So what if we throw a few Divergers into the mix? A few Abraham Wald characters? Remember these could be the same people.

Imagine your team. You have a new problem to discuss. As your colleagues come into the room you ask them to choose a seat based on whether they are a Converger or Diverger. What would happen? If you didn't explain what these titles meant would they tend to follow the first person to sit down? Would they ask you to explain before they made a choice? And then what if you told them beforehand that a Converger was someone who wanted to get the problem solved as effectively as possible; and a Diverger, someone who 'wanted to understand the problem first. What would happen? Where would you sit? So here is a hint or your blossoming Divergers' toolkit; invite people by asking them to attend a <u>question-only workshop</u>.

Hint

Send them a note saying, *'please come to the workshop next week with one question you would like to discuss <u>before</u> the workshop starts.'* And then when the workshop starts ask each of the participants to share their questions with the rest of the group. I call it a pre-workshop question request, but you can call it whatever you like. The important thing is to get people to avoid just turning up and playing the 'I have an open mind' card and to get them to consider what the workshop topic means to them. Not because you want to stifle or lead the discussion but to encourage people to think about how they want to use their time in the actual workshop. And with the prevalence of virtual and hybrid workshops in our immediate future, this simple tactic can be really helpful. Much better than forcing home the 'cameras on' rule because you feel it is respectful.

It might feel a little uncomfortable at first, but the idea here is to help participants to resist identifying ideas and solutions without understanding why they need a workshop. And being blunt, it might say something if no one can think of questions they want to ask. I have run these pre-workshops a few times, and they never fail to reveal hidden gems. On one occasion, we found no one had any questions beforehand. I spoke with the business leader, and we discovered her people didn't understand the topic of the workshop well enough. When she reframed communication with her team they were awash with questions when the workshop was held and contributed to a successful outcome of the task at hand. This tactic helps counteract the bias that often occurs in a workshop. Firstly, it is entirely participatory. Everyone gets a chance to be heard and secondly, it is a pushback to those who dominate the floor.

Workshop wobble

Before I tell you about the wobble ask how you would respond to the question, *'how might we make it easier for people to contribute ideas to solve our problems.'* What does the question make you think about? Do you focus on the 'how might we' words or 'easier' or 'contribute'? And does it encourage you to run a workshop? Now let me ask another question *'when was the last time you were in a really good workshop.'* I qualify the question by saying *'the workshop must have contributed to a positive change AFTERWARDS and not just in the room.'*

Our workshops wobble when they fail to carry the momentum to the days, weeks and months that follow. A workshop that was connected to a flow of collaboration and commitment from within the room and onwards. We wobble when after all the promise and hard work the light goes out disappointingly for all concerned.

And if I had to put down just one reason for this I could have answered with any of these replies; (1) the environment is comfortable and conducive to open collaboration, (2) the facilitator is experienced and able to create fresh energy for ideas or (3) people are rewarded by a competitive culture. Any one of these might be a reason for a good workshop but I doubt they mean sustainable flows of good ideas and contributions. But my answer is *'because we didn't understand how ideas flowed through the people involved.'*

I am talking about trust. In a low-trust environment, it doesn't matter how many workshops, gatherings or away days you run - the outcome will always be the same. Lots of energy and tons of disappointment when good ideas are stifled and not encouraged. But in high-trust environments, you will see innovation flow easily across different teams and units to feed growth. This was of course what the agile lean business model was supposed to ensure happened. But I don't know about you the recipe for such harmony rarely comes from TED talks and mission statements.

How's your flow doing?

Joining a new company wearing the hat of an innovation leader was exciting. My peers in the management group saw my role, as much-needed help to reduce their fragile technological bumps in the road. And so it came about that one day I found myself evangelising to a colleague in Italy about his problems with project delivery. My company-built roads, tunnels, and bridges. I went on to convince him that I had a piece of innovation (software) that would help dramatically reduce his programme delivery cycle - thus saving resources and cash. My colleague, affectionally called Italian Guy by me, bought into this 'evangelism,' and put me enthusiastically into his programme. It was his painkiller moment. I was his hero and it played to my ego.

All was good until the day my innovation fell apart, and I became the pain for Italian Guy. I had a delay on my side. The delay was a straightforward snag that technologists and solutionists like me will nod wisely and say, *'it is just one of those things.'* But for Italian Guy, it wasn't just one of those things. At the end of the extremely uncomfortable phone call, I realised my language didn't work with him. The impact caused by my delay was dramatic, causing his programme to slip and leading to his customer hitting him with significant financial penalties. The resulting tongue-lashing was one thing, but then the brutal accounting rules meant Italian Guy could transfer the 'lost' money (significant) from my budget to his. It was his compensation he told me for the delay with my innovation and led me to cut my cloth very differently for the next quarter, plus a squirmy chat with the Chief Finance Officer.

What went wrong? It would be easy to blame the technology, but the reality was that the problem was me. I had convinced myself I had the 'permission to innovate' with Italian Guy. I used my position and background to influence my colleague without explicitly earning the right to enter his 'town' and build sufficient trust. And this was despite several face-to-face meetings. What is now happening to the flow of innovation in our hybrid world?

Vulnerability based trust

There is an interesting point of view from Geoffrey Moore, a respected author, who suggests any business comprises four zones - called performance, productivity, incubation, and transformation.[60] In his words, the performance zone dealt with sales and revenue, the productivity zone with support - HR, finance, and tech, the incubation zone was where ideas came from (note this) and the transformation zone was for business change and acquisitions.

Moore argues that for a company to be successful with the push for growth it must actively demonstrate vulnerability-based trust between these zones. When I first read Moore's work I immediately went back to Free Guy. What zone were we in as the potential seller? And where did he sit? And most importantly, where did his people sit? And back to workshops for a second. Do we ever consciously look at the audience and consider the zone from which they were coming? Do we consciously select people purely because they are from the same zone and therefore 'on point,' only giving lip service to others out of a form of professional courtesy?

This is hard. Each of these zones will have different cultures, leadership styles, priorities and more. Business owners and CEOs might believe all the zones share the same ethos and purpose, but this isn't always the case. Whether it is because of a silo mentality or very distinct culturally differences, how a business carves up its 'zones' is rarely synthesised as suggested in beautifully crafted mission statements. Individual goals and objectives designed to work in one are likely to cause failure in others. And this is why being a prophet, guru or storyteller entering someone else's zone can be so problematic.

Italian Guy lived in the performance zone, responsible for

'bringing in the money' - in effect, the sales business. I sat across the incubation and transformation zones. My job was to drive the business from a technological perspective while being an innovation catalyst to support change. Sounds plausible and fits the dynamic in most organisations today. Except there were hidden forces at play that were fraught with inter-departmental differences and funding arrangements, typifying the large global multi-disciplinary company that we were.

Assume nothing

What looks good on an organisational business chart can often mask a hierarchy of acceptance and trust. Those neat lines depicting a business's structure and operation hide many sins. And trust is number one in my mind, pulling on the difference between implicit and explicit trust. Lines are often blurred with history, mystery, and fable, portraying one zone over another.

I have sat in management groups where the performance zone takes centre stage, and the sales number is the only 'real' agenda item. A place where the lines of trust with other zones are tenuous, even if polite and respectful. An environment where innovation does not resonate unless a number can be attached to it, of course! I lost count of the times other leaders would effectively say, *'do not come to talk to my people with all your exciting ideas unless there is something in it for them.'* Explaining why many suppliers in the Incubation Zone will attach meaningless financial gains to their 'new thing,' purely to get the attention of performance zone people. Only then to crash and burn when their entire proposition falls apart under scrutiny.

And when we factor in the prevalence of mergers and acqui-sitions, the dynamic between these zones fragments further. A friend of mine sold his small software business to a giant corporation. After a rocky start with largely unsatisfactory results, he would agree in hindsight that permission between his zone (transformation) and the other zones (performance) was not explicit enough to allow him to promote his business sufficiently to his new colleagues. In a small company, it might be possible that these zones all exist within one person's sphere of influence. If you are your prophet and own all the zones, you only have yourself to blame if things go wrong!

We knew that the experts outside our company would point their fingers and call us imposters. So we worked tirelessly to share with them what we were doing and get them on board. Our initiative was effectively a 'free' solution that would make them all heroes, yet they pushed back really hard. Eventually, the sponsors acted, and the solution was deployed. It was so successful that the naysayers soon became our biggest evangelists, singing from the rooftops. A tremendous success, or so we thought.

Delighted with ourselves, the next stop was a full production. This is the point that things started to go awry. The development team shoehorned their team's technology into the solution. When they had finished, we had no idea which sales teams would be compensated for selling the technology. The next part was a huge learning for me. The product was released, but nobody took ownership; as a result, no one in the sales business had the product in their target. The result? No one sold it despite clients needing help in this area.

My learning is to not just rely on your idea or technology is brilliant, that is only half the tale of success. The other is to think about how trust between groups works on the ground.
Claire Penny, Global Digital Evangelist @ Invicara

Where do you sit

I recently ran a workshop with a senior leadership team and tried an experiment. The context was how the team could develop a more courageous streak to innovation and what they could do to generate more creative thinking and problem-solving. I asked each leader to place themselves in the zone they felt reflected their area of responsibility - performance, productivity, innovation, or transformation.

Interestingly, no one put themselves in the performance zone, which seems at odds with their business of manufac-turing and distributing products through channels and directly to customers. But perhaps they hadn't understood the exercise, so I then asked them to put themselves in the zone they collaborated with the most This time, a couple of leaders associated with the performance and innovation zones, respectively. This felt like an anomaly and became a discussion point. Did they think that innovation that affected performance, sales and customers was someone else's remit? And if so, what about innovation in their zone? How did they ensure they were working as a team? Despite the *'bon esprit'* in the room that day, there seemed to be a lack of vulnerability to experiment and be courageous with ideas that could help others. Of course, such a discussion is only a glimpse into someone else's world, but it was interesting to peel back the onion slightly.

I encourage you to think about the point of view of looking at zones and innovation in the same thought process. Explore your situation and see if you can identify how your business is structured and more importantly, how innovation flows across people from different zones. What is the mechanism to allow this to happen successfully? It might be the annual workshop, the daily stand-up meetings or entirely reliant on water cooler serendipity. But there is a hidden zone as well. Every company has one. It is just that it doesn't show up on organisation charts or job descriptions and it is this zone that does undermine innovative thought.

The pressure zone

It would manifest itself usually 24 hours before the end of a sales quarter. Or the night before a management board. And then magically disappear soon after. And when I am in the pressure zone, but you are not, then the chances of a successful conversation about innovation - or anything else for that matter - are marginalised. You might have a ground-breaking money-saving idea that I would be foolish to ignore, but if you talk to me while I'm in the 'zone' - well, good luck. And the difficulty is that we don't know we are in the pressure zone because it feels like it is all the time, right? I reflect that the management group struggled to identify with the performance zone because they felt every day they were in the pressure zone. Does this resonate with you? Because the other aspect of 'which zone are you in' is the most damaging one of all - the person who speaks the loudest.

The loudest voice syndrome

We all know this phrase, *'Let he who speaks the loudest have the last word.'* And whilst I am sure we don't concur with the sentiment it has been part and parcel of business life.

In my time, the 'loud voice' would be sales leadership, who would carry the weight of the 'number' and worry about anything else destabilising people from the call of duty. These individuals would overpower discussions about 'new things' with gusto saying, *'look time is against us so let's pick it up next quarter.'* And once the loudest voice has spoken the room would fall in line, leaving the 'innovator' effectively the last person standing. Daniel Kahneman, the father of behavioural science wrote, *"the standard practice of open discussion gives too much weight to the opinions of those who speak early and assertively, causing others to line up behind them."* [61]

If this is true how can leadership create a mechanism for all voices to be heard in a psychologically safe manner, even when people are sitting across all these different zones? I have no data on this, but I wager that one of the reasons why so many innovations fail is because of this point. We may have all seen people lose faith in grand transformation plans where innovative ideas were signed up and invested in when they see little emotional support from those above. And when leaders themselves lose faith and distance themselves from the vision, the innovation does indeed die. Sound familiar?

So I want to talk about three tactics of psychological safety that I have used when working with teams who admit they have a problem with making innovation work for them. And they have absolutely nothing to do with technology and all to do with trust and flow between zones.

Create tension

Tension in a low-trust situation is toxic and can ensure everyone feels they are in the pressure zone all the time. But the tension in a high-trust situation is a positive experience that allows people to feel vulnerable to share ideas, concerns, and issues without fear of being mistreated and undervalued. We should use tension to encourage diverse opinions and ideas because when we do we challenge our biases and assumptions.

Imagine we are about to discuss *'ways to make our streets safer at night.'* And imagine there is a line drawn across the floor in the room. At one end stands the perspective that *'surveillance cameras make me feel safe walking home,* and at the other, a perspective that *'I resent being spied upon by faceless authoritarians.'*

Now you are asked to stand at the starting position closest to your personal view on the matter. And then when everyone has had a moment to flow around the space positioning themselves, they are all asked to share their rationale. And then after a round of discussion, the group is asked to reconsider their position on the line seeking compromise and understanding. I have seen enthusiastic discussions come from the 'line exercise,' which blows away the cognitive cobwebs. An icebreaker I would use before a discussion about innovation and solving business problems is that can improve how people contribute and pay respect to each other for differing points of view.

Tension is a thing to be embraced in an environment where trust is open and appreciative of vulnerability. And in low trust situations do you know what happens with this line exercise? The group will stand next to the person who carries the most seniority and speaks the loudest. When this happens, and we can all imagine our own experiences here, any innovative talk is dead in the water.

Challenge distraction

The second tactic comes from Jeff Bezos, Amazon CEO. It is said he starts each meeting in total silence as those present read a memo outlining the context of the discussion about to take place. Then with laptops closed and phones turned off, they discuss the memo – all at precisely the same time.[62]

This is a great example of 'working alone together.' I recall many management meetings where such a tactic would have helped tremendously. Those times when people would arrive un-coordinated and un-prepared, citing burning platforms inside their pressure zone as their mitigation, leaving you to doubt the reliability of their cries for leniency and more time. And if you were the person invested in the idea, it would become a nagging frustration that even though your colleagues were physically 'in the room' with you, they were cognitively absent that day. Distractions are the death knell to innovative thought. I wonder how many good ideas failed to make the grade simply because not enough people were paying attention on the day the idea came to town.

The truth is in our modern world we like being distracted. And many warned us that it was going to cause us harm. Aldus Huxley wrote in Brave New World Revisited, *"the development of a mass communication industry, concerned in the main with neither the true nor the false...failed to take into account man's almost infinite appetite for distractions."*[63] And is the level of distraction a growing barrier to our ability to give innovation a chance? And perhaps more tellingly what is our environment like to support good ideas?

Where do ideas come from?

When asked to think back twelve months and identify ideas that have had a positive (or negative) influence, the team I was working with, struggled. They wanted to dive into the creativity that the workshop promised but I wanted them to take a moment and reflect first. Yet I wanted them to look back and challenge each other about where the flow of ideas came from. I encouraged them to identify the sources, characters, barriers and opportunities for why this is so. I explained that before they launched an 'ideas fest,' it might be useful to know what their track record looked like. And when they did they identified some assumptions that were not valid which helped them consider who they had in the room.

Hint

I call it a Good Ideas Audit. Look back at ideas that have changed your behaviour positively in the last 12 months. It might be in your personal life or business. They do not have to be earth-shattering or technology-related, just ideas that have influenced you. Now next to your thoughts, think about the source of the idea. So were all the ideas yours, or from partners, colleagues, or your boss? Did they come from outside, perhaps from a consultant, relative or friend? Or did they just appear as something else and magically morphed into something more useful? Then reflect on what you see. Consider the zones they come from i.e., do the majority come from the Incubation zone where you might expect them to? Is there a pattern in your circles that point to good ideas predominantly coming from one major source? Or is it more sporadic and general? And what about good ideas that ended up being bad ones? Anything to see here?

A Good Ideas Audit is a very enlightening thing to do before you embark on discussing fresh ideas for innovation. It will make you think about who you have in the room and if there are patterns of behaviour and obstruction that you need to be aware of. Pop in the Diverger's toolbox?

Functional fixedness

PepsiCo faced the problem of too much sodium in their potato chips. They originally looked across their industry for ideas faced by competitors and engaged external consultants to 'get innovative.' But their most creative ideas didn't come from this approach. No, it came from an orthopaedics department that had undergone research on nanoparticles of salt to tackle osteoporosis which allowed PepsiCo to lower the salt in their product. [64] This describes a bias we have known as <u>functional fixedness</u>. A bias where we see an object as only capable of meeting its original purpose i.e., a hammer is for banging nails into the wood not for stopping papers from blowing in the wind, a blanket is for keeping warm not for children to build a playhouse with - and a smartphone is for calling people up and texting, never to be an oil tanker!

And with the oil executives, the playtime abstracted their problem, distilling it down to the fundamental components. By eliminating the details of their challenge they were able to think more creatively about the solution. The exercise stopped them from judging ideas too early in the problem-solving process and helped them consider alternative perspectives and outlier ideas. Something they would never have done if they had followed their usual corporate frameworks and methodologies. A classic Diverger's tale. It is why crowdsourcing is now so popular as a platform to generate fresh ideas that come from outside a business, to draw in fresh ideas that come from quite different minds and to rule our preconceived biases from inside.

Please, trust me

I have talked quite a bit in this book about trust. I do so quite deliberately because with Free Guy I now realise we had a low-trust conversation going on. Weirdly, I say this because at the time I would have said the level of trust was high. After all, they were an existing customer who had placed business with us before. (first mistake) and the chit-chat with Free Guy and his leadership team always seemed friendly and open (second mistake). So when we decided to bid for the work we felt confident we had a strong chance of winning (third mistake) based on our perception of the trust relationship we thought was in place. And when I then went to work with bigger tech firms I witnessed the 'brand trust' misnomer (fourth mistake) where we believe because of 'who we are' the door is wide open.

Trustworthiness is defined as *'the ability to be relied on as honest or truthful.'* And according to Charles Green, there is a way to consider how good you are at being seen as trustworthy. The Trust Equation suggests that trustworthiness is something we have to think about consciously if we are to make positive and open progress in a relationship.[65] But how many businesses rely heavily on their brand as the 'trust card,' without really putting in the effort to consciously consider how trust might be influencing the conversation?

When written down, the Trust Equation looks like this,

$$\text{Trustworthiness} = \frac{\text{Intimacy} + \text{Reliability} + \text{Credibility}}{\text{Self-Orientation}}$$

First, you need intimacy between the people involved. This a fairly obvious thing to say, but a factor taken for granted in our fast-paced world. If I share something in confidence with you, I expect you will protect the information and do nothing to embarrass me. Then you need to show reliability so that the output of an interaction with someone else will be honoured and not left wanting. If I said next Tuesday, then you must deliver next Tuesday. Or if you said the costs were X, then they should not become Y. And finally, you need to prove you show credibility with what you are saying. Your advice and skills must be demonstrable and proven to have material substance to the discussion at hand. And below the line, you absolutely must show a low level of self-orientation where you listen and show humility to the other person. Often the hardest thing is when we believe we have 'just the thing' to help someone and we just can't wait to tell them all about it.

Italian Guy revisited

When I replay my Italian Guy experience against the Trust Equation, I come out poorly. First, I embarrassed him through my eagerness to be innovative, disregarding his relationship with his customer and what was at stake for him. I then lost the reliability and credibility in the relationship by missing the deadline and being unable to demonstrate my idea was fit for his outcome - not mine. It was all about me, my thoughts, and my network of supporters. As a result, my self-orientation was too high, thus lowering my trustworthiness. I recognise that I didn't want to appear vulnerable in the conversations with the Italian Guy. I, therefore, pulled on my intellectual arrogance to mask this and now recognise this behaviour in many others who feel they cannot appear to not be in control.

Call me naive, but how often do we look back at failed innovation conversations to explore why they might have failed? Do we focus intently on the technology and market opportunities only to disregard how 'we' behaved with each other? Do we sidestep conflict because we feel it will slow us down and prevent us from flagging opportunities which is key to how we are measured? Are we taking too much for granted that undermines our recovery from a situation?

It was not until the paramedics tried to move me that the severity of my accident started to become clear. I had just been hit by a motorbike courier who had been overtaking the standing traffic. I had sheered my pelvis in half. My recovery was slow, from months of bed rest to a wheelchair, hydro pool and then a Zimmer frame. I had to learn to walk again. I tried to live normally, but the pain kept coming back. Painkillers got stronger, and the gaps between visits to the chiropractor got shorter.

I knew I had to rebuild my muscle memory to find a sustainable way to manage pain and allow me to live again. A doctor to whom I will be eternally grateful recommended Pilates, from which I have never looked back and, ten years later, continue to practice. No painkillers are now needed!

This dramatic event has shown me that the businesses we now support believe short fix shots in the arm will stabilise their culture and direction of travel. The truth is, however, that just like my Pilates classes, a business needs to commit to developing its muscle memory to build trust and collaboration across teams. This will deliver sustainable growth. It is tough, but the rewards are tenfold!
Vicky Reddington, Founder, The Amplified Group

Innovation is crucial to everything we do - but you can't get sustainable innovation without trust. Somehow in our conversation, we have to work a lot harder to make sure we have enough trust in place to allow innovation to flow. Yes, this can be helped through having a workshop culture, recruiting Wild Ducks and external gurus and spending money on research but it will only be effective if trust is demonstrated openly between leaders, teams, and zones.

The simple tactic of conducting a Good (Bad) Ideas Audit is not the answer but it can be an honest appraisal of where you have come from and might indicate blind spots that have prevented progress as you might have wished.

When we converge on our problems we assume trust is present. And when we do we also assume conflict and commitment can be managed to ensure all involved are accountable to get the intended result. I have seen people believe that just because they work for a big brand name they don't need to establish where they sit on the trustworthiness level. Or maybe fancy-sounding job titles do it? The more senior a person the more they must be high on trust. You will have your version of this no doubt. But in a finite game of selling and buying this is an incredibly dangerous place to operate if there is a distinct lack of open and vulnerable trust. According to Patrick Lencioni, author of Five Dysfunctions of a Team, *"Great teams do not hold back with one another. They are unafraid to air their dirty laundry. They admit their mistakes, their weaknesses, and their concerns without fear of reprisal."*[66] Yes, Vicky Reddington, I did finally read it!

It will take our Diverger self, therefore, to challenge and disrupt to ensure we create the trust necessary to come together to work on the real problems and solutions that were hidden from the low-trust Converger behaviour.
This chapter might have gone around the houses on innovation a little, but I wanted to expose the vulnerability we all face when talking about fresh ideas. We might hold bean bag-laden workshops with all the razzmatazz you can ask for, but if we haven't taken the time to understand how trust and ideas flow, we should not be surprised when

workshop fatigue kicks in and people vote with their feet. As Brené Brown wisely noted, *"vulnerability is the birthplace of innovation and creativity."*[67] No matter how amazing an idea might feel or how compelling a strategy seems unless we are thinking about the human element - psychological barriers and trustworthiness.

We build clever shortcuts into the technology we take for granted - think satnavs, online banking and perhaps, facial recognition. All is done to save us the brain power to think for ourselves saving our energy for more important things to think about. All done because it is inevitable that humankind will repeatedly find innovative ways to survive and thrive. The last leg of the trilogy of temptations - speed.

Innovate or die

CHAPTER 4

GO FASTER, SLOWLY

"Life moves pretty fast. If you do not stop and look around once in a while, you could miss it."
– FERRIS BUELLER

A man pulls a child's red truck down the middle of a street. Inside the red truck were ninety-nine smartphones. What happened next...?

Each smartphone ran Google Maps, sending its location to the internet giant's 'cloud.' The anonymised data was interpreted as showing a lot of traffic - moving very slowly. It transpired that Google could not distinguish between a child's red truck full of smartphones and a genuine traffic hold-up. [68] The man pulling the little red truck, Simon Weckert, was playing a trick on the internet giant. He wanted to prove a point that we are biased towards believing what we see, even when it is plain wrong.

Otherwise known as the 'computer is right' story.

Trust in what we see on our screens has less to do with technology and everything to do with our desire to smooth out bumps in our journey - like traffic hold-ups. In Weckert's experiment, one wonders how many car drivers re-routed their journey because of Weckert's gimmick. How can we place such blind trust in a dumb piece of equipment? There may be many reasons but fundamentally it is because of our desire to be smart and agile. And even when we get slowed down by 'a blip,' we continue to think we were right and refuse to change our loyalty to the tech. Especially if we have paid for it. Sound familiar?

The computer is right

Hundreds of employees were complicit in the fraud, so said the computer. And as a result, many were prosecuted, declared bankrupt and sent to prison. Except that they were all innocent. The computer belonged to the Post Office and was developed like all systems to improve and optimise operations. Yet the Post Office management could not rationalise what the computer screens were telling them versus evidence to the contrary that hundreds of employees were part of a scheme to defraud them. They were anchored on the information they could see shutting off rational thought and reason.[69] A situation that haunts many businesses that trust the technology to speed up what they do, at the expense of taking a step back and slowing down. As historian Joshua Rothman puts it *"The real challenge isn't being right but knowing how wrong you might be."* [70]

And the faster we go the risk of not knowing how wrong we might be increases. Of course, we know this but yet we still find examples like the Post Office story everywhere. Is it because of the poor design of the technology? Perhaps? Or is it more likely that we cannot admit we cannot cope?

The dilemma of speed

In 2011 an article in Forbes magazine spelt out the dilemma many in business faced. The authors interviewed business leaders' who considered what was on their minds and returned with a universal feeling that *"we try to match complexity with greater complexity and speed with increased speed. Feeling out of control, we seek more control. Instead of the clarity we crave, we get ambiguity and more uncertainty."* [71] But now in 2022 surely this outdated situation has passed? Or is there still relevance to the words echoed by the business leaders a decade ago?

The urge to go faster might be the primaeval characteristic of fight or flight influencing our thoughts. It might also be the FOMO effect (fear of missing out). Or both. Either way, we worry that slowing down does not align with our goals and dreams and might be construed as hesitant and obstructive by others. And the clever people - whoever they are - who produced the correlation between speed and 'smart' have been doing a good job at reducing our fears.

Smart = Speed

Put the word 'smart' in front of anything these days and the assumption is that you mean things will speed up. I don't think there is anyone out there promoting a 'smart' product that advocates a slowing down of an outcome. After all, no one bought a smart TV so they could take longer to find their favourite show, a smartwatch that didn't work with our online diary or a smart water bottle that didn't help our hydration.

In my research I was astonished by the amount of 'smart things' we talk about; smart grids, smart motorways, smart law enforcement, smart energy, smart water, smart foreign policy, smart golf balls, smart pencils, smart motorhomes and on and on and on. And of course - smart kids!

It seems being smart holds no bounds and feeds into the trilogy of temptations that speed is the outcome. I remember the early trials of something called 'smart dust' - tiny micro electromagnetic systems that could detect movement, light and sound quite useful in the context of warfare but now useful for fertilisation and pest control. And in China you will be able to 'smile to pay,' making physical cash or plastic redundant, letting your face do your expression of satisfaction.[72] Can you imagine the implications of such innovation? What was the problem they were trying to fix? Are people so tired of waiting to pay that they want to remove all possibility of friction? Or is it a scheme to improve happiness in a retail setting? And what about security? What if your smile doesn't unlock the transaction on a 'bad day'? And will your bank issue 'non-smiler' violations and block your account?

And on a grander level, I am sure as taxpayers we are funding ''smart weapons' and many still pursue the vision of a 'smart city.'

It's the smart thing to do

All of this 'smart' talk transcends the physical products we design and reaches into all facets of political and social life. Have you noticed that when leaders want to create momentum for an idea, they will often frame their speeches using the language of smart, *'if you don't follow me then you will be doing the dumb thing?'* Do you remember President Obama saying, *"empowering women isn't just the right thing to do, it's the smart thing to do?"*[73] It is as though just doing what is right is not enough anymore and that it has to be smart to make a real difference. A form of coercion I suppose that suggests if you don't take the smart option then the only route left is the dumb variety.

Online social media is increasingly being used to rank behavioural traits that could determine the likelihood of being hired. One example, originally reported in the Washington Post, described an 'automatic babysitter ranking system' that was mining the Internet for content to produce a risk rating for prospective babysitters. [74]

For example, scoring from one to five (where one is the best, and five is the worst) on a range of factors such as likely to take drugs, likely to be a bully, and likely to have a bad attitude. One candidate had her chances thrown into doubt when the AI scored her a two instead of one for some aspects, despite passing criminal background checks and a face-to-face interview. With no information or context supporting what she may have done to fail to achieve the perfect score, the parents began to doubt her suitability.

What have we become? There are a host of issues with this trend. For starters, behaviour analytics to profile individuals based on their digital data traces is barely better than crystal ball gazing. It lacks the context that is needed to explain behaviour, given most occurs in social settings. What does a score of 2 instead of 1 on a measure of 'respect' even mean? There is so much potential for AI to enhance and extend our cognitive capabilities. But that opportunity will be lost if we forget what it is to be human in the process.

Sharon Richardson, Behavioural Data Scientist
(adapted, with permission, from 'Is the use of AI dehumanising behaviour') [75]

We can all blame the smartphone for our modern-day dilemma of 'smartness'. It was IBM neatly thirty years ago who invented 'Simon' - the world's first smartphone. [76] The smartphone was a device that could be both a phone and perform computing functions. And when we started to design technology that could reduce the effort on humans to 'think' the die was cast. But has this almost pathological desire to insert 'smart' into every conversation taken away plain old common sense and logic? What happened to 'dumb' if that is even the right thing to describe 'life before smart'? What have we become indeed? Lazy? Arrogant? Or are our wisdom and foresight making our lives easier to live?

Or have we become so converged on creating solutions to help us speed up that we are sacrificing common sense and privacy? Many questions sit at the heart of our ability to think logically (or not) about how we solve problems today.

By stepping away from the old ways of analogue life through the automation of everyday tasks we are relieving our brains from needing to remember. When we learn something new, our brain creates a mental bookmark of the information, available to download in the future, as and when we need it. A convenient way to allow us not to have to remember the firehose of information we are consuming. We know these cognitive bookmarks are 'in there somewhere' without us understanding their context and story. But at what price? If you were to imagine how colourful our brains were millions of years ago, you might be right to think they were blacker and whiter than our modern variety. Our ancestors would have 'simpler' problems to deal with, albeit often a case of survival or not. Now shades of grey infiltrate our busyness, forcing us at times to press the 'Go' button, believing we know the answer already. And when we do this we skim the surface of what we know about a topic, simply to show others that we know more than we do.

On your bike

We have likely ridden one as a child and into adult life. Even my attempt recently, after a good 25 years gap at least, saw me staying upright. But please do not ask me to tell you how one works!

Studies have looked at a phenomenon that suggests we just don't know enough about everyday things - or as much as we say we do. Like riding a bike. In one study, participants were asked to draw a picture of a bicycle. [77] To ensure that lack of artistic skill was not a factor, they were asked to view images with different arrangements of chains, pedals, and frames to state which corresponds to a working bicycle. The result was that half the participants could not do it. A number drew bicycles that would be completely non-functional, i.e., missing chains, no seat, no brakes!

And it is not just bicycles. When asked to rate knowledge of such mundane objects - toilet flushes, dishwashers, micro-waves - people would tend to rate their comprehension high but would then fail miserably to explain how they worked. We think we know many things but do not know as much as we thought.

What I am describing is a bias known as the Illusion of Explanatory Depth (IOED), which fits well into the thought that in our haste to go faster, we over-egg our knowledge of a subject. [78] Just think about past job interviews. Or when as a teenager, responding to parents offering you advice you would wisely respond '*know, I know, I know.*'

Hint

Play your own illusion game. Pick an object with which you are familiar. It might be a physical thing like a kettle, or a system thing, like the stock market. Give yourself a score out of ten on your understanding of how you believe it works. Higher for really confident, lower for less. Grab a colleague or friend and get them to do the same. Now explain to each other how your chosen object works. Then mark yourselves again after reflecting on how your description sounded when heard aloud. How has your scoring changed? Are you more confident or less? Did you learn anything from your colleagues' stories that might influence your level of knowledge? Then take some paper and try drawing out how the object works. Has that changed your scoring again because you fail to identify a key component or process? Try a few different objects, then sit back and consider what this might tell you about your illusion of knowledge radar. Reflect also on what this light-hearted exercise says about how you approach more serious subjects that might have more serious ramifications.

If we can build tightly coupled systems such as the Airbus 380 aircraft capable of flying between London and Sydney in one flight or producing 3D printed tissue to mimic the heart's elasticity, it is reasonable to believe we can go faster. And everyone is at it. Scientific thinking is no longer the purview of those industries that have had centuries of learning and research. Now industry as a whole is immersed in scientific analysis of their markets, customers' behaviour, and digitisation of their products and services. The days of recruiting leaders with 'home' industry experience are changing. Now businesses will parachute leaders from disparate industries wearing T-shirts emblazoned with *'we eat transformation for breakfast.'* The logic is that If you can prove you transformed a manufacturing process at scale, then it is given that you can re-energise a charity organisation to do similar. And whilst all this bears the hallmarks of the right thing to do, how are we individually coping with the pressure to demonstrate that we know enough?

Not so smart, eh?

Be honest are you one of those who is happy to stand up in a business meeting and say, *'I'm sorry, I just don't know enough.'* Despite what we might think people do not want to hear this. Politicians wouldn't get the vote and lecturers might find empty classrooms. And I don't think I would feel great if the Airbus 380 pilot or heart surgeon whispered such words in my ear.

The reality is we don't like to admit our vulnerability, especially to people we don't know. We will go to extraordinary lengths to mask our depth of knowledge to avoid people thinking, *'she doesn't know as much as she should.'* And when the culture around us is one of 'go, go, go,' the fear of saying we don't know can be debilitating. And it all comes down to trust. In a low-trust environment, not being able to let people open up about their vulnerabilities, is only going to spell trouble further down the line when accountability and collective results are demanded. Whilst in a high-trust environment being able to share vulnerability openly can be the gap that leads to a successful outcome.

Where am I going with this? I am trying to show, that in a world where speed and being smart dominate the conversation, the illusion of knowledge factor is also increasing. Why? Because our memory is not like a movie reel playing in one continuous stream, but instead a reconstructive process requiring constant rebuilding; which is why sleep is a key factor by the way. Our memory needs a regular workout which is why I like the Bicycle test because it reminds us that thinking we know about something doesn't mean we know it well enough. And when it's not bikes but something relevant to the conversation we are having we run into problems of our own making. And when we are with others who also have the same 'colourful memory' we can very quickly reminisce about what we think is happening whilst losing the essence of what is really happening.

Groupthink

I am talking about Groupthink. A situation when a group of well-meaning people make irrational decisions believing they are on the right track often made worse because others expect them to know more than they do. A characteristic famously articulated by Donald Rumsfeld when he declared *"as we know, there are known knowns; there are things we know we know. We also know there are known unknowns; that is to say, we know there are some things we do not know. But there are also unknown unknowns - the ones we do not know we do not know."* [79]

The design of business and government - hierarchy, rules, and compensation - can enforce the groupthink mindset. You might now be thinking of your groupthink examples. Was groupthink the problem for Abraham Wald and his US

113

Air Force colleagues? Was it a trust issue or simply a blinkered observation caused by groupthink or anchoring on what they could see and not what they couldn't? In our quest for answers quickly to win harmony and conformity driven out the ability for an individual to speak out and say, *'I don't agree here'* or *'I don't know enough yet'*? My hotspot was the 2016 Brexit vote that spoke to the risks of a binary scheme - in or out - built on a quicksand smorgasbord of illusion. If there had been a third box labelled 'don't know enough,' what would have happened? When faced with 'complex' subjects like constitutional and climate change and all things cyber - the risks of our illusion clouding the outcome can mount up devastatingly. With no box for 'I don't know' and only 'yes or no' on offer, the pressure to conform has both good and bad sides. The good is all about feeling safer and wiser; the bad is all about being frightened and uncertain.

The problem with security is that those of us who do it for our jobs often believe we know what it means for those who have to use it to do theirs. It took me to take a step back from doing 'security' to listening to those who did not. I now run an Ambassadors program, where we primarily discuss security themes but consciously put ourselves in the shoes of the people that we are trying to help. Working with this group of volunteers, I gain wonderful insights into the different lines of business and how to harmonise cybersecurity efforts with the most pressing needs. This empathetic group continues to thrive and evolve and is one of the most rewarding things I have ever done. The worst thing we can do is to think we 'know' what a solution should look like without getting the confirmation of the people we aim to serve.

The most notable change in behaviour is the willingness of users to report issues and ask for help. This has led to more false positives than before, but it is great to see that users would rather be safe than sorry. Another satisfying aspect of this is seeing the level of trust that we have managed to build up.

The motto of my security awareness initiatives from day one has always been: 'alone, we are smart; together, we are brilliant!'
David Mantock, Chief Information Security Officer, SPIE Switzerland

When slow met fast

Who likes speed bumps? Is it just me or are they getting higher forcing cars to slow down even more? And who has the job of deciding where they go?

Increasingly our lives are mixing the slow and fast as we layer on top of what was there before with what we want to see. One only has to look at how we repurpose old industrial buildings into residential neighbourhoods to witness this phenomenon. London's Battersea Power Station from the outside still retains the look of a power station facility whilst inside is becoming a modern destination for communities to live, work, eat and play. The lower layers - concrete, brick, steel - from the original 1940s design (the slow), now provide an interface for refurbishment, creativity, and transformation (the fast).

There is a quote that could well be the equivalent of the *'mind the gap'* sign on the London Underground. Stewart Brand, the American writer best known for the books, Whole Earth Catalog and How Buildings Learn, would talk about *"the fast parts learn, propose, and absorb shocks; the slow parts remember, integrate, and constrain. The fast parts get all the attention. The slow parts have all the power."* [80] Brand was referring to the interplay of how nature, culture, governance, infrastructure, commerce, and fashion all move at vastly different speeds. Brand believed it is the contrasts between each layer that figures out how successful or not the upper layer will be. It is these contrasts or gaps that lie in the opportunities to design new experiences and better outcomes. And in these gaps lies one thing not often discussed too openly in the drumbeat of selling and buying but was no doubt on the mind of Free Guy - namely, legacy.

Legacy load is real

He was the technology director at a UK library and had just told me about his intriguingly titled, *'legacy load index.'* His job was terrific. He had oversight of some 170 million items of all manner of printed and digitised formats. On his to-do list was the digitisation of entire websites for Middle East nations, while protecting the Magna Carta and Leonardo da Vinci's notebooks. His world consisted of hardware and software that read like a veritable Who's Who of computing architecture. A legacy that would not have looked out of place in a science museum or an episode of Antiques Roadshow. He looked after systems that no longer had any living subject matter experts who knew the inner workings of the technology, nor anyone still in business making the vital spare electronic components to keep systems alive.

What I loved about this guy, let's call him Legacy Load Guy, was his pragmatism. His grand-sounding legacy load index was a mere spreadsheet but was the best way he could visually show his peers the risks they were taking in their decisions. He presented to them each month the reality of a system having no one alive to support a failure and the implications for the smooth running of the library. Here was a business leader confronted with the trilogy of temptations. His customers demanded fast through the high-speed technology available, but he also kept a watchful eye on the slow using technology of yesteryear. He sat across the gaps between fast and slow, i.e., the material - systems, the equipment, and the messy, i.e., the people, the shadows, and the workarounds. And it wasn't just him. His whole team carried this ethos in subsequent conversations.

I repeat this story when speaking with others interested in how they should approach transformation through technology. I use it to help them describe their version of fast and slow in their own business. A sort of temperature gauge of what they are up against. A gut reaction. And to get them to stop, think and describe what they do to bridge the slow and fast with 'something.'

And it is the 'something' that I find quite fascinating. Because knowing what it is can be the secret sauce to keeping things going fast and slow. I just can't tell you what the ingredients of the sauce are!

Hint

Imagine your <u>legacy load index</u>. In business, we all have a legacy, no matter how trendy and current we think we are. Perhaps the buildings we occupy are old, the equipment we use is creaky and the processes we follow are clunky. And the people? Some set in their ways, others bursting with fresh ideas and vigour. And suppliers might be in the groove with technology, while others are still using the quill pen. There may be traditions and myths that build up a legacy that your business or industry is this way or that. And fond stories that resonate remarkable feats by people long gone. Legacy load is a real thing. We all have it. So the hint is to take a minute and consider what it might look like. A moment to reflect that at the speed you are headed and whether there is sufficient due care and attention taken to the legacy. You might find, like Legacy Load Guy, a way to quantify and measure your index and keep an eye on the glue that keeps it all hanging together.

I want it NOW!

Theodore Levitt claimed, *"People don't want to buy a quarter-inch drill. They want a quarter-inch hole!"*.[81] This a much-used phrase to illustrate the importance of delivering an output through a process, but In my mind tells only half the story. I would say that whilst people might think they need a quarter-inch hole, the real reason is that they have a painting to fix to a wall. And that painting just happens to be a family portrait they hope will lighten the room and bring joy to those present. And whilst we cannot expect designers of 'input' technology that we use in whatever way we choose - like Free Guy in fact - it does not excuse them from thinking about outcomes and experiences. And I forgot to mention - we want that experience right now. Why wait?

My guilty pleasure is the marshmallow. Pink or white, I don't mind. And if there is a bag of said deliciousness anywhere near me it will be a brave person to try and stop me from eating the lot. What I do know is I would have been a weak candidate in research undertaken to examine this behaviour. The research took a group of children aged between four and five years old and offered them a marshmallow choice. A researcher placed a marshmallow in front of each of them and told them that if they did NOT eat the marshmallow while she was out of the room, they would get a reward of a second marshmallow. However, if they ate the marshmallow while she was out of the room, they would not get another one. The research found that many children grabbed the first marshmallow, but intriguingly, several did delay thus receiving the second reward. The interesting anecdotal follow-up was that when followed up in later life, those children who delayed their reward, appeared to do better in educational results.

Gratification - friend or foe?

How good are you at waiting for something you think you want? Do you become so impatient that you will compromise on a better outcome in the future just so you can get pleasure right away? And would you say your use of technology reflects your gratification meter? Happy to be offline or can't imagine that situation? This describes the irrational and subjective human trait called <u>instant gratification,</u> which is *'the temptation, and resulting tendency, to forego a future benefit for a less rewarding but more immediate benefit.'* [82]

And when we seek instant experience we compress all of the DBOFO stages into a hormone release to get the O for Outcome right away. Think social media but also binge-watching TV or real-time business reporting. And even our language mirrors this desire for instant gratification when we exclaim *'I'm back-to-back today'* and *'I'm so busy that I will catch up on sleep at the weekend.'* Why? Because everyone else is speaking the same language and if we don't, then they will think we are not team players or someone who can't keep up. Sound familiar?

I tried extremely hard to make friends with my brand-new shiny, fancy tablet. There was just one problem, my hand-writing looked awful, and I had zero satisfaction. I realised I was taking fewer and fewer notes. I lasted about a month and then went back to clandestine notetaking by hand (when I could get away with it). It raised a host of questions for me, though, why do I insist on continuing a habit that could very legitimately be seen as inefficient? Would I want to go back to letter writing by hand? (Absolutely not - typing emails is most certainly more efficient than writing letters).

Then it clicked. Tech is a tool. Typing is efficient for communicating quickly, I understand. For me, though brooding over a case, a puzzle, or a contract, I need the scratchy feeling of a pen imprinting my thoughts and theories physically. Underlining things I have not yet grasped, drawing, and visualising (euphemisms for my doodling) is satisfying to me and creates an imprint in my memory that still is present even 20 years later. I am convinced there is no digital way of replicating this experience (yet!).

What does this mean to me as a professional in a digital setting? My love for the pen taught me to be more respectful of how people function and be more empathetic. There is more than one way to achieve a common goal.

Carolina Souviron, Head of Legal and Compliance, Swisscare Group

And as a footnote to this thread about gratification; there is a wonderful publication unsurprisingly called Delayed Gratification that is all about 'slow journalism.'[83] I won't spoil it but if you like the thought of slowing down and reflecting on big news events through the power of data visualisation storytelling, then this might be your thing.

When we diverge our thinking and delay our gratification we can spot interesting things lying in the proverbial gaps that were there all the time. Like missing bullet holes.

Marginal matters

The CEO of SAS Airlines, Jan Carlzon, faced a failing business but rather than do what logic suggested he diversified his thinking and thought small. Or marginal to be more accurate. His story was transformational. Carlzon inspired his people to change their mindset by saying *"to succeed in business and differentiate yourself from competitors, you do not have to be 1000% better at one thing; you have to be 1% better at 1000 things!"* [84] Rather than go for substantial changes to recover his business, Carlzon was going the other way. He successfully arrested the decline of his airline and encouraged others to apply a marginal mindset. When British cyclist Bradley Wiggins won the Tour de France in 2012, his success was partly inspired by marginal change. His coach, Dave Brailsford, paid attention to the marginal differences like finding the best pillow for increased sleep, getting into the design of the bike seat, optimum tyre weight and personal hygiene habits. [85] Today, industry and sport routinely use the language of 'marginal' to frame problems in easier ways for people to consume.

It is funny because for a large part of my career no one cared too much about marginal gain. It was all about big strides, significant jumps, and substantial change. All right I know I was in sales, but we can all reflect on leaders' banging the 'think big' drum.

Why do we have this desire to 'over egg' the pudding? I was working with a client who faced a challenge in how to share files between two data centres about sixty miles apart. This was in the days before fast links, or the cloud was an option. Our proposed solution was technically sophisticated but expensive - about £250,000. My technical engineer and sales manager - the client included - all of us knew that in less than six months, super-fast communication would be available between the two sites. This was always going to be a temporary fix.

Maybe it was my Scottish Presbyterian upbringing, but it bugged me that they should have to spend so much on something that would be surplus to requirements so soon. It just did not feel right. While sitting in the CIO's office, I had an idea. The data that needed to be shared between the sites daily was the equivalent of two large magnetic tapes. Silly as it sounded, could we not use a motorbike courier instead to transfer the files between the two sites once a day until the new super-fast link was installed? It could be done for less than £150 a week, a little more if we wanted weekend cover, too. Happy customer indeed, but I now had to explain to my sales manager why my forecasted £250K deal would not be coming that month. I was not in his good books. But before you start to think, Isobel, you missed an opportunity there... months later, we secured a purchase order for over £1 million as the first phase in replacing this customer's mainframe.

Would we have won that business anyway? I will never know. But I learned a valuable lesson that has helped me on numerous occasions. Do not overcomplicate things, do what's right for the customer, and always keep it simple. Put your customer's interests first, and it will be appreciated.
Isobel Rimmer, Founder, Masterclass Training

There was a time - maybe still is - when businesses were described as speedboat and tanker businesses. Speedboat businesses could swerve in and out of obstacles accelerating ahead to find new markets, while tanker businesses were set on a fixed course, hard to manoeuvre but powerful and resilient. The difficulty arose when leaders who advocate a dual strategy to their people yet fail to realise that their troops at times were unable to jump back and forth between the speedboat and the tanker.

Free Guy knew his business was trying to be a speedboat - his entire industry was on a path to acceleration. His real problem was not how to train them to adopt the new technology but was about getting them to understand how to operate in a culture that was both speedboat and tanker. In a nutshell, his dilemma was *'not how to speed them up but how to slow them down first, and then speed them up second.'* Sounds counter-intuitive, doesn't it? But doesn't this just sum up the challenge? It isn't a speedboat or a tanker that people need. They just needed a boat. Or is it a ship? I always get that mixed up.

The antidote to speed

Heard this one, 'two ears one mouth.' We all suffer from not listening enough as we seek to speed up. I might not agree with your point of view on a matter, but if you are genuinely listening to me, then I will feel more positive about working with you - even if I think my idea might be the better one. Yet when under pressure to deliver results it is increasingly a risk that we don't listen enough to each other causing unhealthy conflict further down the line.

Why is this so important and why does this have nothing to do with technology but everything to do with you and me?

Because before we can decide that what we need is a 'captainless speedboat (or tanker) powered by AI and 'smarts,' we have to retain our curiosity to first ask, Why? Not in the obvious ways of identifying our problem and seeking a solution, but in a deeper understanding of the impact on the outcome.

It is as if we are playing a game of snakes and ladders. The ladders promise us so much that we are tempted to climb as many as we can - as faster as we can. But as we do we have a nagging thought that for every ladder we climb there is a snake to slip down too. We might think we are sufficiently curious and open-minded to accept the risks and rewards but as Hal Gregerson puts it, *"answers are more valued than inquisitive thought, and curiosity is trained out of us?"* [86]

The rest of the book will now explore how we get back this 'lost curiosity' and rediscover how to have the conversation we know we need. And it starts with the problems we think we have.

Go faster, slowly

CHAPTER 5

FALL IN LOVE WITH PROBLEMS

"The mind is like an umbrella. It's most useful when open"
- WALTER GROPIUS

In the Southern Indian state of Tamil Nadu, children were born malnourished, too weak to fight illness, and tragically dying. We might reason that famine and poverty were the cause of this, but that is only partially correct. The expectant mothers were starving themselves because they feared pushing out a big baby would damage their health. Aid agencies spoke to pregnant mothers to explain the dangers to their children of being born malnourished, trying to understand their anxieties and motivations. Based on their research, they designed a programme to supply extra food and continuous reassurance to the soon-to-be moms. And it worked. Fewer babies were born malnourished, and many more survived infancy. It was not surprising, therefore, that when a comparable situation appeared in

Bangladesh the same tactics were deployed. The results, however, were disappointing. Unlike the experience in Tamil Nadu, the mother-in-law controlled the family food intake, diverting the extra food to their son and the expectant mothers continued to be deprived of nourishment.[87]

The Tamil Nadu and Bangladesh stories describe wonderfully how hard it is to be a Converger and Diverger when we think the problem is the same as one we have seen before. The aid team undoubtedly diverged on getting under the skin of the problem for the mothers-to-be. They would have used empathy and curiosity to find a viable solution. And yet when they were in the Bangladesh region they converged on the answer because they had a readymade solution - or so they thought. And the lesson is to never underestimate the mother-in-law!

Solving problems is cranky at times

Problems. We are particularly good at finding them but less successful at understanding them deeply enough. We focus on what we can see and dismiss what we cannot.

At one time or another, every business leader and their customer will have said, *'please just solve the problem, so it stays solved.'* No one likes to find they have to take a step back when they thought they were taking two forward. But as we all know, all it takes is a problem we haven't thoroughly investigated to show its hidden and often ugly side. I am talking about framing and reframing problems; something our brains execute hundreds of times a day.

And technology helps at every turn to convert everyday tasks into habitual clicks and flicks to help us rationalise and reroute our decisions accordingly. But the stuff going on below the surface is the worry. Those things that pop up spoil our plans and we cannot easily change direction. As individuals, we know what these look like - the dripping tap that might mean something sinister under the sink, strange withdrawals on our bank statement, or the colleague who does not respond to time-sensitive requests. What we must do is consciously explore patterns and structures below the surface to understand what is going on in case they represent more of a threat or opportunity. And to do this, we need to acknowledge the space the problem is occupying. In effect, do we understand the context of the problem enough or are we only looking at it one way?

The problem is space

How do you hold your smartphone when taking a picture? Is your photo library largely made up of portrait snaps with only occasional landscape views for special events? This unconscious experience feeds our muscle memory of how we view information. In a portrait view, we can take in what is happening in front of us, but what if something is interesting going on around the periphery of our vision? And when we switch our view to landscape, we see the problem space. And when we do, we see the mother-in-law - and the missing bullet holes.

Conventional problem solving naturally focuses on the 'average user,' using the theory that if our solution can solve their needs, the rest will follow close enough. This suits our Convergers mindset because it means we can move on to the next problem confident we have solved the problem as best we can. In contrast, when we diverge, we actively seek 'extreme participants' from the start, challenging the average and the norm. By including both ends of the spectrum and not just the 'average,' a full range of behaviours, beliefs, and perspectives will be included. The mother-in-law sat at the edges of the average hidden from portrait view and only visible when seen in the landscape. As Robert Sapolsky, neuroendocrinologist wrote, *"if you pay lots of attention to where boundaries are, you pay less attention to complete pictures."*[88]

When we face a problem for the first time, we go through a mental checklist of understanding based on previously known facts, assumptions, and biases. This behaviour will converge on the problem as we see it often with our heads down and not looking up and around at the surrounding problem space. And in business, when on the pitch of the finite game, we will often sacrifice time to consider the problem space, believing we have the answer already.

Been there, done that

The job was to design a tunnel. A tunnel that would bypass the city of Stockholm - suffering from terrible traffic delays, vehicle pollution, and debilitating citizen well-being. Our mindset at the time was locked into our belief that *'we knew all there was to designing tunnels.'* A belief that was derailed when the client walked in and said, we could only be successful when we understood 'really why' the tunnel was needed. And so a few days later, each of us went on car journeys around the city with parents doing the school run, drivers dropping off parcels and taxis picking up fares. We spoke with cyclists, elderly in mobility scooters and pedestrians. I even spoke with traffic control officers and a man on a horse. After two days, the entire team reconvened having completed numerous journeys and conducted hundreds of interviews. The problem had not altered- they still needed the tunnel - but now we understood the problem space much better. Up to that point, our evidence around the problem had been quantitative based on what data we could see - how long it took to drive across the city, readings of pollution levels, and how long vehicle queue lengths were at rush hour. But what we didn't have was qualitative insight from the perspective of the people who mattered the most - the city's citizens. After our experience, we were better in-formed about why we were doing the project and how the design would materially impact the lives of the citizens - not just the average but also those we couldn't see.

Think about the other person

What I am talking about is known as the study of human behaviour - otherwise called ethnography. When we stop and think about the other person, we consciously try to be in their shoes, understanding their intentions, motivations, pains, and gains. A study of their journey in effect, from where they are and where they want to be. A study that observes their interactions and touchpoints inside their problem space, searching for ways to improve their situation. A study that does not just use one source of knowledge but is open to considering multiple, often conflicting evidence to shake out known facts, biases and assumptions that set the scene for us to consider different answers than we might have done before.

Why are elevators SO slow?

We have all experienced slow elevator syndrome at some point in our lifetime. The experience of staring at the button, pleading for it to be our turn to escape the uncomfortable sensation of silence from being so close to others and that disturbing body odour we can smell.

Now imagine you are that person faced with the problem statement to find a way to *'speed up the elevator.'* In the portrait view, they can see the practicalities of the engineering upgrade. But what if taking in the landscape view they realise it is more about human emotion? Initially, they might have started by asking the question, *'how might we make an elevator travel twenty per cent faster.'*

But when they reframed into landscape view, taking in the emotions of the human involved, the question *'how might we make riding an elevator twenty per cent more enjoyable'* became more interesting. This is why we find mirrors in lifts today. Yes, mirrors. You see the mirror allows us to use the dwell time to check hair, straighten wandering ties and just feel less claustrophobic in a metal box with strangers. The mirror gives us distractions from the feeling of time lost and vulnerability from strangers. All because someone reframed the problem by thinking about the problem space (human emotion) and not just the problem itself (engineering effort). Emotions, not motors, vulnerabilities, not cables.

An interesting footnote is that one of the prominent elevator players, Kone, rebranded itself from being known as a lift and elevator manufacturer to becoming a people flow specialist. A pivot influenced by pressure from their market to influence human-centric experiences and remove bumps in the road for people getting to and from places.[89] Another DBOFO example surely?

Disruption can be fun

Imagine you and I both work for ACME PLC's customer services department. Our boss has just given us this problem statement, *'the sign-up process is far too long because customers are making too many mistakes with security sign-up. Our support desk staff are having to field more support calls than optimal. We need to rewrite the website to fix the problem.'*

Now look at these three reframed statements below and choose the one you think may have the best chance of producing a desirable, viable and feasible solution to the original problem stated above.

A – How might we amend the website to improve data accuracy from the customer sign-up process

B – How might we help customers feel they have all the information to share with us successfully

C – What if we stopped customers from failing to identify three sources of identification when completing the sign-up process?

Think about the original problem statement. Was the

language too closed, suggesting a possible solution, i.e., the website, the login process, the security questions - shutting down any other contrary ideas? And what about the reframed problem statements - A, B and C?

Problem statement A is anchored on what ACME needs to know, i.e. more accurate data. But who says a website is the best route to collect this data? Who is to say this data is what we need as well? And what about the customer? How would they benefit from a possible solution? Will it be easier and more convenient for them or is the problem statement framed more towards ACME?

Problem statement B is more biased toward the customer having the resources to provide the 'information to share with us.' So, on the one hand, the empathetic language - *'help customers feel'* - suggests more focus on the person who matters the most. But the implication that the website is still the collection route does potentially block 'some' from successfully sharing their information because of their circumstances i.e., not everyone is online or digitally savvy to navigate websites. And what about language and the visually impaired?

And problem statement C? Does it too lack empathy with the customer and focuses more on the ACME problem? By drilling down onto the security aspect of authenticating to the website does this statement increase the bias that only some of the customers will benefit from the solution? And does problem statement C contain too much of a solution i.e., *'three sources of identification?'*

What if we then throw the three problem statements up against the wall and apply the Trust Equation? Which one offers more trustworthiness? Problem statements A and C appear a little more self-orientated, focusing more on ACME's issues and not the customers' experiences. Problem statement B feels credible by concentrating on the customer and not ACME, but then what about intimacy? We are talking about customer personnel information collected by a website so is there a risk that we might redesign the website, and enhance the security process, but create a low-trust relationship with our customer - just when we thought we were doing the opposite?

What we don't ask

Don't forget it is often the questions we aren't asking in our problem statements that reveal the 'real need' and may lead us to the best solution. And who is to say that the website process is the best solution? Does it contain bias from people who are anchored on their problem i.e., we have always had a website so we will always need a website? Problem statement B at least offers a possible compromise solution, which reaches more customers whilst improving the data accuracy and increasing trust between ACME and their customers.

The ACME problem statement has holes all over it and I have only picked a few. How we reframe what we originally identify as our problem, can help us think about who, what, how and why. Questions we say we always consider when challenged by others to think outside the box but are blindsided by our tendency to forget to ask.

How does this help you?

I am describing a problem-framing technique called, <u>How Might We.</u> Using the words How Might We forces our brain to open up and actively ignore previously considered constraints. Think of it as using an eraser. So in the case of problem statement B, the use of How Might We framing opens up the possibility that we don't might need a website to collect the information and opens the possibility that we don't even need to collect any digital data. When we reframed using problem statement B, our minds opened to want to know a lot more about the customer, their feelings about sharing information, the type of information they are asked to share and what the outcome might be for them once they have.

Writing or defining problem statements can be hard work. We tend to be too broad or oversimplified, like, *"how might we redesign train travel?"* or *"how might we create the perfect train carriage made of disused aircraft fuselage?"* could be too broad or too solution orientated. Whereas *"how might we redesign timetable information displays?"* might encourage us to think more about the passenger's experience - their pains and gains in effect. This reframing exercise is intended to disrupt our thinking and keep our minds diverged as long as possible before we rush towards the 'Aha' moment. And when we feel we have a good grasp of the problem and the space involved, we can start diverging our thoughts to seek the best solution. By asking a series of <u>What If</u> questions to challenge the FAB – facts, assumptions, and biases – our brains can be prised away from preconceived ideas.

Prepare to reframe, reframe, and reframe again

Back to the ACME example. Consider this new reframed statement, *'how might we help staff show customers how easy it is to complete the sign-up process the first time.'* Now we are considering the staff - and the customer - widening our view of the problem space. We are now thinking about them by shifting the emphasis onto the staff.

Perhaps the best answer is not how to help the customer but resides with the staff, *'what if we give staff a reward,'* *'what if staff were on live chat with the customer.'* Or *'what if we showed a video of a well-known soap TV star completing the sign-up process?'* Or more dramatically, *'what if there was no website'?* Now we are stretching our minds away from our assumptions that a website is part of the answer. Why is this important? Before doing this, our logical approach might have been to remain anchored on *'customers making too many mistakes'* and produce a solution neither desirable nor feasible for the customer, but also not viable for the business. By using the What if framing technique we are opening our minds to consider diverse options, no matter how crazy they seem, giving us time to consider and debate without our judgement clouded by what we thought we knew was right.

Problems provoke emotion

Ask any medical professional and I am sure they will

confirm that eliciting from patients what the real problem is, can be a tricky business at times. Despite best intentions, the real issue can often be buried inside incidental details that distract us until it is too late i.e., *'my head hurts but only when I banged it on the ground. Why? Oh, because I was up the ladder when it happened. Why? Because the chainsaw I was using to cut the hedge went a bit crazy in my hands and I couldn't hold it because my arm was already bleeding quite badly.'*

Imagine the impact on the team's emotion in mission control on April 14th, 1970, when the Apollo 13 crew announced, *"Houston, we have a problem"*. [90] The stunned silence in the room that followed must have been palpable. Suddenly a problem was on their desk that forced them to challenge their understanding of the problem space to find the solution. The record reveals they successfully did, of course, but only after hundreds of reframing How Might We and What If discussions - and a lot of coffee, no doubt. A valid collective response to challenge everything they previously thought they knew.

The popular adage, *'a problem shared is a problem halved'* might sound feasible, but we may reflect on times when this is not true. I might be interested in your problem statement to a point because I am a colleague or a friend but may be less invested in finding a resolution when considering my problem stack or time constraint.

Humans are funny like this. I will stimulate different emotions in you when I tell you I have a problem, and then when I explain a solution to you. The adage *'don't give me problems, give me answers'* kicks in here. In business, we are sometimes hard-wired to deflect those who appear to only 'create problems' and lean into those who are 'resolution finders.' And when we do this invites even more Convergers to the table at the deference of the Diverger who might just have a feasible alternative idea. In truth though, rarely are we all on the same page when discussing problems. And this is why we need to find a way to fall in love with problems to find the hidden opportunities that lie there.

During the first national lockdown in the UK, online grocery delivery slots were booked weeks in advance. So supermarkets started to do random "drops" of delivery slots to deal with this situation and be equitable. Now, if you wanted your groceries, you needed to hit the jackpot. I was not happy with spending my time locked up inside my apartment, refreshing their website constantly for the grand prize of some pasta. So I tried to find ways to automate this repeatable task. I wrote a simple script that would ping my supermarket's website every five minutes to check if a slot had appeared and sent me an email when it did.

It was immediately helpful for me, and, pleased with myself, I put out a tweet explaining what I had done. A few strangers reached out to me and expressed interest in being able to use the tool for themselves. I did not have much going on, so I decided to put my product development skills to effective use. I contacted friends who also had experience building software products, and we built a simple website (findadelivery.com) that would let people enter their postcode and receive an email with a list of slots as soon as they appeared on the supermarket's websites. I asked other friends to try it, and then I shared it with colleagues at work and on Reddit. The response was fantastic! We quickly grew to hundreds of users across the country. The feedback was touching - from people with mobility impairments to the mums of colleagues. The simple service we created as a fun project was making a difference.

This was a valuable process to go through because it made me reconsider what is "essential" when building products, and it taught me the importance of moving quickly to solve a problem.

Karan Navani, Product Manager

If I had to think of three words to describe how to rejuvenate the approach to problem-solving, I would say 'explore,' 'experiment' and 'encourage.' To explore the problem space to see if known facts, assumptions and biases are understood, or if 'missing bullet holes' are somewhere to be discovered. To then experiment with reframing the problem statement to see what shakes out. And then encourage others to embrace the discipline of diverging their approach by putting themselves in the shoes of the person with the problem.

We treat problem-solving as an inbuilt capability that doesn't need any conscious health check. I disagree. There is more we can do. Which is why I often advocate to teams to run what I call 'Bullet hole and mother-in-law workshops.'

Hint

Grab a few colleagues who are interested in exploring and experimenting - and choose a common problem that everyone can at least understand the context, like 'fly tipping.' Discuss what the problem is from the known facts, assumptions, and biases. Like *'the cost of fly-tipping to each taxpayer is £X,' 'the household bins are not collected frequently enough'* or *'it is always the people from the housing estate that do it.'* Then try and reframe the problem using How Might We, so for example, *'how might we make it easier for people to dispose of their unwanted household items.'* Practice a few of these to get the hang of it and ask people to vote on their favourite one or two. And then try the What If technique. Get people to throw out as many ideas as possible to the How Might We problem statement liked the most, i.e. *'what if we paid people to take their rubbish to the refuse tip,* or *what if we ran classes to show people how to repair their household items*?

Encourage everyone to put forward ideas without judgement or selection. No idea is a bad one. Our goal is to find the hidden bullet holes or the mother-in-law. With a feast of ideas to go at then ask people to vote on the What If statement they like best. Don't set any rules. Just let them go with their head, heart, and gut reactions. Some will try to rationalise; others will go with emotion. Take a step back and see how you could move onto problems closer to home.

To truly fall in love with problems requires stepping outside our comfort blanket of rushing to the solutions, keeping our minds open to absurd ideas or anything that seems radical in pursuing the best answer.

The Paradox mindset

Contradictions are where problem-solving does get interesting.

How often do you discuss problems where there is often a straight-line path to resolution that people expect you to follow? Terrence Deal and Kent Peterson would comment, *"in much Western thought, puzzling situations are considered simplistic problems with predetermined answers rather than puzzling dilemmas begging for a balanced judgement."* [91]

Who has not uttered these words at some point in their lives, *'this is the beginning of the end,' 'save money by spending it,'* and *'do more with less'*? These phrases make no sense from one perspective, as they contradict each other but exist to point out the truth. Studies suggest that people who thrive on learning to embrace conflicting demands show greater creativity and productivity. They lean into situations that pull them simultaneously in opposite directions that, rather than creating tension and stress, build curiosity and diverged thinking levels. [92]

Paradoxes are uncomfortable as they challenge us, and business leaders are often very keen to eliminate them, explaining why we are encouraged to think in absolute terms – yes/no, A/B, right/wrong. Attempts at quantifying preferences to simply one answer might seem sound from the questioner's perspective, but fail to capture the intensity of human emotion, *'my Yes might be different to yours.'* And inside these responses lie the blind spots and opportunities that business leaders often try hard to ignore because they suggest uncertainty and ambiguity.

And when the goal is to go faster, win bigger and remove bumps in the road, encouraging such thinking is not always top of mind. But we must learn to disrupt these biases, not to be awkward and obstructive but to offer diversity to the problem-solving process. To this point, consider the statement, *'do we train people for today or tomorrow?'* Is it enough to have people you trust to help you solve problems today, but who are not the people you need tomorrow when the problem spaces change? And if you emphasise tomorrow do you compromise what you need to achieve today? This a classic paradox that many leaders ponder frequently.

To fall in love with problems we not only need to be open and diverged to see problems differently, but we also need to step into the shoes of the person affected the most.

Empathy - our secret weapon

After the Haiti earthquake in 2010, people from around the world rallied around raising money and sending clothes. Nancy Douyan's family were affected by the hurricane, and she remembers, *"If you step outside of your pain, you will realise that during an earthquake, people are not thinking about clothes. If you looked into it even a little bit, you would have known that there was a cholera outbreak and that there was not any clean water."* [93] Our urge to want to help, step up and solve problems completely blindsides our view of the space a problem resides. And as we all know, when news comes at us like a speeding train as it does these days, we often anchor on the first thing we see to build our response. A quite natural response but leaves us no time to put ourselves in the shoes of the person we are trying to help.

Called 2G Tuesday, Facebook would encourage their developers to *'slow down their phones'* to experience what it would be like for a customer in a low bandwidth area.[94] Similarly, Ford would get their designers and engineers to wear 'empathy suits' to understand what it must feel like for a pregnant woman to get behind the wheel of their product.[95]

But other businesses without the depth of resources and time will assume and anchor customer experiences by taking shortcuts in research and development. The tactics of the 'average' would be their play, often taking huge assumptions in their understanding of the person they were expecting to help.

I mentioned earlier in this chapter the discipline of ethnography, where researchers observe the traits and behaviours of a specific demographic, community, or group in real-time. Ethnography is qualitative, focusing on obtaining first-hand and high-quality data directly from the source, making the knowledge more substantive and outcome orientated. Ethnographers aim to get 'under the skin' of a problem.

They hope that by doing this, they will be able to understand the problem and, therefore, design a far better solution. Ethnography is not about collecting vast amounts of data about a cluster or segment of people. Nor is it a mere matter of running surveys or questionnaires. Ethnographers are all about understanding the other person and spending time with them, listening to them, and watching how they do what they do.

What is your version of Facebook's 2G Tuesday or Ford's empathy belly? How do you go about living in someone else's shoes? Do you have a conscious process of understanding the issues and fears of the people you are hoping to help? Do you have specific activities to challenge your view of their problems and experiences? Or do you tend to rely on research from others focused more on quantitative rather than qualitative knowledge?

On a recent new build Healthcare project, a design team presented their computer-aided layout and elevation drawings. There were 3D models and engineering schematics that visually addressed the client's statutory and specific requirements for a new build inpatient ward facility. Although the technical and clinical members of the project team had studied the drawings, there were still several fundamental flaws that were not addressed. This included locating a separate plant room adjacent to one of the wards' proposed fire exits. A structure that would have prevented bed-bound patients from being safely and quickly evacuated whilst remaining in their beds during an emergency evacuation. The outcome of this fundamental problem would have been disastrous if not spotted. Once identified, the technology made it simple to rectify the problem in the digitised planning documents.

But I could not stop thinking we were missing something. We might have created a digitally collaborative solution that addressed all design parameters, but it had not considered the person's experience in the bed. From their perspective, the view from the window was effectively a brick wall.

Whilst technology and innovation are making buildings quicker, easier, and safer to commission, the teams need to not just accept their work as being compliant but importantly also consider the needs of the people who are looking out of the windows also.
Mark Williams. Director, Boardroom Knowledge.

Ethnography is a discipline that is a long way away from the bustle of the finite game but is increasingly in demand. Why? Because the business world is now waking up to the realisation that to win the finite game means they have to embrace the infinite too. And there is work to do. Despite what they think business leaders are facing a 'drought' of diverse thinkers in their organisation; people who can win the game but win it with fresh perspectives and curiosity. And one of the inherent skills they are desperately seeking is helping their people 'fall in love' with the problems their customers are facing.

Why did they do it that way?

Netflix. If you had asked me before I would say Netflix is

about streaming someone else's content, producing their own and doing it all via a subscription model. A simple-to-understand model that is not unique. But do we know why they do it? Not for obvious reasons like paying dividends to investors or compensating their people or actors starring in their films. Look at what they say, *'to entertain the world. Whatever your taste, and no matter where you live, we give you access to best-in-class TV shows, movies, and documentaries. Our members control what they want to watch, when they want it, with no ads, in one simple subscription.'*[96]

And then I read about Suzi Lu, a data visualisation engineer with Netflix. and when I first read Suzi's story, I asked myself why would Netflix need data visualisation engineers. Were they not an entertainment broadcaster, not a data company? Then I read some more. Suzi was a curious type and was *'compelled to think of ways that data visualisation could be used to redesign everyday experiences, and the receipt was the idea I was most excited to play with first.'* [97]

Yes, the receipt. A product of our physical world that stubbornly resists the digital age by turning up in our pockets and bags. Rarely do we give them a second glance, retaining them for claiming business costs, or just in case we have to return an item - a mundane piece of transactional evidence that contains little or zero value. An annoyance that digital tech has eradicated from our lives.

Curiosity doesn't kill the cat

But not for Suzi Lu. The receipt represented a transaction,

and given she worked for Netflix where transactions were the lifeblood of their business model, she was curious to see if she could change the perception and value of that humble piece of paper. Suzi asked, *'how might we make the receipt more useful to the recipient.'* And began to build prototypes against a frame of *'what if we made the information more interesting to look at.'* Without changing any of the physical components - the thermal printer, paper, and transaction information - her prototype grouped items into genres i.e., how much were spent on food versus alcohol versus kitchenware. Suzi was experimenting with how visual cues could influence human behavioural change. She was fully in her Diverger mindset. Since then when I see a Netflix email alerting me to a new film or box set I think of Suzi Lu and the Netflix mission statement.

They aspire to *'entertain the world'* for *'you'* and *'our customers.'* The entire mission statement is all about <u>us</u>, not Netflix. They want to make as much money as possible, who doesn't, but that is not what they are saying. Between their words and Suzi Lu's prototype, I got a glimpse into how human-centric thinking mattered most to Netflix. Of course, they are not alone, and I could list other brands that have the same approach to understanding the problems facing their customers. But what the Netflix story taught me was to be more curious about *'why people do what they do.'*

Hint

Grab hold of a mission statement of a company that

interests you and do a bit of your own 'Why' investigation. Perhaps you want to get a job there, sell them something or want to invest in them. Or they are the creator of your innovative thing. Take a minute to digest their visionary words and jot down keywords that stand out for you. Words that perhaps focus on customer experience and service orientation. Or a narrative that makes a solid commitment to sustainability and supply chain evolution. Or is their language all about them and not the people they are helping? Remember the Trust Equation and the importance of low self-orientation?

Now find someone who works for that company, as I did with Suzi Lu at Netflix. LinkedIn is my default source but there are plenty of others out there. Maybe someone in the news who works there. Now look for people who are sharing original ideas and perspectives. Someone who appears to be an individual with an opinion but who also is amplifying their company's mission. Like Suzi was doing. Try and avoid researching just the CEO or leadership because you might get a 'canned' copy.

The goal is to see if you can find a correlation between their company's mission statement and what people who work there are saying. Do people amplify why they do what they do - not just what and how they do it, i.e., launching product X or promoting event Y. Or do they add their narrative to amplify why this is so important to the reader? Do they discuss problems in their world and share stories of success (and failure)? Are they showing a vulnerability to their work that gives an insight into how they think about their customers' problems? And if you find one person, go, and look for others. Why? Are you witnessing an outlier who might be a Diverger in a Convergers world or might there be a culture of diverged thinking that might give you a glimpse into their Why?

━━━━━━━━━━━━━━━━━━━━━━━━━━━━━━━

I hope this is resonating because I now want to dig deeper into the human factor - or the person who matters the most. I say this because too often we jump to conclusions that we understand the other person and therefore, in our conversations, we create these blind spots and illusions in how we think we can help.

The challenge, of course, is how we think about the other person with the problem who matters the most when we can never be that person. Instead, we rely on research by others who have already put in the hard miles, grouping and segmenting people with similar problems and aspirations. I would inwardly groan at sales campaigns that would target senior roles in specific industries i.e., Chief Finance Officers in insurance or CIOs in the public sector. It was as if people with these titles would have the same problems and therefore would be comfortable talking about your products. I know it was a tactic of the finite game of selling, but too often it just made no sense in my mind. The entire exercise took on a numerical perspective that completely dismissed any attempt to help the seller understand the actual real person with the title. I felt that when these campaigns came around, they would lack any differentiation and would treat the person who mattered the most - the customer - as if they were all the same. But I have played this game, so I am guilty too.

At the time, I would not have cared about what Free Guy was thinking. My job and that of my team were to get his signature on the deal that he wanted and had chosen my company to deliver. He had asked us the questions - we had gotten them right and the deal was to be signed. It was as simple as that. But was it? If I had my time again and knew what I have learned during my career, I would try harder to understand his problems. Not from within the words on the procurement paper but from trying to step into his shoes - or to see things from his perspective.

If I were to think of that meeting again, I would want to ask the questions below.

- What are you <u>thinking</u> about this deal?
- How is the proposed change making you <u>feel</u>?
- What are you <u>saying</u> about the expectations of the deal?
- Do you think you should be <u>doing</u> things differently?
- What <u>fears</u> do you have about this change event?
    - Can you describe the <u>gains</u> you expect to see?

Empathy Mapping

What I am describing is a component of a human-centric technique known as <u>Empathy Mapping</u>. The underlined words are the trigger points to encourage the listener to reach into their emotions and share their feelings. And it is a tactic that for the Diverger in you can be incredibly powerful to expose assumptions about the other person in the conversation.

The groundwork for asking these questions would rely on a level of trust between the two of us to speak this way. It would not be too wise to consider such questions where trust is too low or nonexistent. This a point I often ask people to think about when preparing to meet someone for the first time. What might sound good in theory can crash and burn when used inappropriately.

Why can this be so powerful? Neuroscientists claim that pleasure and pain are processed in overlapping regions of the brain and work in a state of equilibrium. The more we experience pleasure, the balance tips towards the rewards we believe we will receive. But we have a self-regulating mechanism that strives to return the balance to a level state, like a set of old-fashioned kitchen scales would do. This seesaw unconscious event is why empathy is such an important aspect of really understanding the other person, but one that is dismissed in the hustle and bustle of playing the finite game.

The Empathy Map questions are an attempt to quantify the responses the other person is having about their problem nudging into their pleasure/pain unconscious thoughts to reveal something inciteful.

Spoiler alert

I know many sales leaders who would dismiss such an approach as way too subjective and theoretical. They would claim this is not an approach that can be scaled, is fraught with subjectivity and is open to more bias and misguided interpretation than the hard-coded approach. And they make a fair point. And our dear friend the Pareto Principle backs up their thinking. If we can win the game by getting eighty per cent of our success from twenty per cent of our customers then let's keep it tight and not get too deeply involved.[98] And for sellers with ever-expanding targets, patches and compensation twists and turns the incentive to 'be empathetic' is a tough gig.

I would counter by saying that in Free Guy's case this was a person who when confronted with a specific business event - signing off a deal with absolute constraints and deliverables - used language that was steeped in vulnerability and contradiction - *'even if it was free.'* I would argue that when we push away titles, hierarchy and business logic, everyone has an Empathy Map that waiting for someone to help them expose. And no one wants a column in a spreadsheet with the heading 'Empathy ranking' - yes, no, not a clue.

But what if (see what I did there) we could be simply curious enough to want to exercise our empathy side? Might it reveal something we did not know about the other person that might lead to why they are behaving the way they are? I recall a wonderful story about an old woman being asked to show how she found opening her pill bottle. She took the bottle out of a drawer, put it on a meat slicer and calmly sliced the lid off the bottle. She suffered from arthritis.

Push away what we thought we know

When we show empathy we synthesise our observations of

the other person's emotions, fears and hopes. Using this human-centred approach encourages us to push away our assumptions and illusions about the person and their situation. This is not sympathy but something different. Empathy is about connecting with the other person, instead of trying to find an appropriate response because we think we know what they are experiencing. Empathy is not about 'getting on with them well,' but about prising open our minds to receive new information.

When we do we are only thinking about the other person - not ourselves. Our attention is switched to listening, observing, and inquiring, hoping to spot an opportunity to help them. And the Empathy Map is a manifestation of this cognitive habit. The maps can be done in one's head or written down, done solo or in groups. What you are looking for is empathy with the other person. It is not a scientific process and will not reveal 'the answer' like a magic trick. No, this approach is an attempt to open up your mind to consider what the other person is experiencing. It is just one tactic that when we diverge can help reframe the problem we thought was on the table.

Hint

The next time you prepare for a meeting consider the person opposite you and create your Empathy Map. Write down the headings - think, feel, say, do. Take a moment, turn off your distractions and consider the emotional state of the other person soon to be talking with you. It might be just one person or a room full. Try and do this without judgement. Now consider what you put down. How might these words influence your approach to the candid conversation with the person you are thinking of? Then think about the pain the other person might be experiencing (with the situation) and what they hope to gain (from the situation). Don't worry about getting this right because you can't - that's not the point of the exercise. What the empathy map does is give you the space to think about the other person. And do you know what? The empathy map can be an excellent talking point with the other person. If you feel there is trust between the two of you why not? What is the worst that can happen? They tell you what they are thinking feeling saying and doing and where their pain and gain sit. Isn't this a gold dust moment in a conversation where there is mutual respect?

How do you help someone feel more connected and trusting of the space they are in, particularly if it is somewhere completely new to them? We can, I am sure, all relate to this experience and how much we dislike taking out our phones and looking intently at the screen or listening to the instructions we are being told to follow. It disrupts our experience! What then if you were blind or visually impaired? The challenge would be enough to make you not want to go out at all! But...what if there was a way where you would, more naturally, know what is around you and where to go to make your way from one place to another? This was the challenge a team at Microsoft Technology and Research took on. The key to the approach they took was to design with empathy and compassion and draw on our natural human abilities to process information in an inclusive and empowering way. The thorny question we had to figure out was not a technological one but how we were going to shift thinking away from the locked mindset approach of giving guidance through navigation technology and moving a person's perception toward an experience which offered greater awareness of one's surroundings. And it was this change of thinking that led them to a place where they use sound to create an intuitive experience where anyone can explore while feeling at ease and empowered.

Soundscape simply works by calling out places around you from where they actually are in relation to you - so that you intuitively build a mental map of a space. The team were driven by their curiosity and desire to learn from everyone, including people with blindness, and were able to challenge the bias of prescriptive guidance being the only way to navigate a space, and along the way, we're able to demonstrate the value and impact of purpose-driven technology.

In a way, it has become a metaphor for how technology might look in the future, in terms of how value is retained inside and as part of a human experience. Soundscape embodied this idea and really has stretched our thinking on how value can be transmitted through a completely human-centric approach that not only gives control to the individual using the product but also opens up a channel through a diversity of ideas for others to build on and extend and uncover fresh new opportunities previously hidden away.

Linda Chandler, Microsoft UK, Industry Lead – Smart Places & Soundscape advocate

Prospective hindsight

To close this chapter there is one more hint I want to share with you. I call it <u>prospective hindsight</u> which works on the principle that something you are planning to do has FAILED. Yes, that's right; something you are about to do that you believe will work but has just FAILED.

You are planning a wedding, big sales conference, or business case pitch to the board. You have completed all your tasks, thought of everything and the green light is on. Confidence is high and the risk of failure is low. But before you press the button you invite fellow collaborators to a <u>premortem workshop</u> - a contradiction to a post-mortem where you examine what happened. You ask the assembled team to consider the reasons why the future event failed.

There is one rule for the premortem workshop - everyone has the opportunity to speak. They are asked to explain why the event failed to deliver the desired outcome. There is no judgement nor attempt to challenge and clarify. This exercise is about being transparent and open.

<u>Hint</u>

Consider a solution to solve a problem that has been agreed upon but has not commenced. Announce to the people involved that you want to run a premortem workshop. Ask them to spend a few minutes in silence considering the reasons why the solution failed. Go around the room and ask them to roll back from the anticipated outcome and identify how, what, and why it FAILED. It might be due to technology, outside influence, or a skills gap in performing a task. It could be anything. Ask them not to narrow their reasoning but encourage them to think as widely and crazy as possible. Encourage them to think of their review in terms of a person who is involved with the problem.

Technology is the easy bit. It didn't use to be like this decades ago when we were distrustful of computers and preferred things as they were. But figuring out the problem in the first place seems to be getting harder. We are in a world of 'technology abundance' that seems to overwhelm our ability to cope. And remember whilst you and I might feel we can cope it is about the other person. Like the old woman, her pill bottle and her meat cleaver. How are they coping? What pain are we inadvertently causing them by assuming they are doing okay?

But perhaps understanding the technology and our problems are not where we should start; perhaps the real problem lies in our ability to ask the right questions in the first place. Are we conveniently asking questions that people expect us to ask, because of the pressures and numerical constraints of the finite game played? Are we substituting our natural inquisitive side for quantitative outputs that one day could be programmed into Terri and Tobi - running 24 hours a day, without pay and emotion? And then what will we do?

CHAPTER 6

THE POWER OF INQUIRY

"Raking is easy, but all you get is leaves; digging is hard, but you might find diamonds."
— *JOHN PIPE*

In my childhood, learning was primarily measured in absolute terms - right or wrong. Students would be marshalled within a frame of reference outlined by curriculums, mock papers, and teacher guidance. Learning to be right was already infiltrating into young elastic minds and onwards into the world of work. Soon meeting targets, achieving compensation, and job security mattered more than being interested and curious.

The pressure of delivering results and hitting targets reduces our brain's ability to take a moment to think about what is happening. Instead, we tend to dumb down on what we can see in front of us, pulling down from our mental bookmarks answers and solutions that fit. Mainly because we believe we do not have the headspace to press the pause button and because we believe others will not thank us for saying, *'hang on, give me a minute to think about this.'*

Being inquisitive is tiring work

Asking inquiring questions hijacks our brain. Once a question is out there, we find it hard to think about anything else. Questions open up (and close) pathways in our brains that, like an itch, become irritating until it goes away. When asked a challenging question, our brains race to find the best answer. Usually at the expense of any other thought process.

Workshop overload is a real problem. Whilst it is positive to bring people together to tackle a problem collaboratively and openly, it can also be overbearing on the 'grey matter' if the process itself becomes the barrier. And on top of this many business leaders are wary of spending too much time on open and challenging questions, no matter how cool and exciting they might sound. They will complain that 'too much inquiry' can drain their ability to maintain focus on the day job of winning the game. It is simply too exhausting for them to keep up and will privately say, *'why can't they just keep it simple.'*

Leadership tough love

Being in leadership is a difficult place to be. On the one hand, they have to win the game they are on the clock for whilst maximising the skills of their people to not only win today's game, but tomorrow's too.

But I do feel on balance there is a shift away from leveraging the inquiring mind of their people towards a more 'colour between the lines' approach. As Francesca Gino of Harvard Business School puts it, *"although leaders might say they value inquisitive minds, in reality, most stifle curiosity, fearing it will increase risk and inefficiency."* [99]

Leaders will tell me of their fear that people will 'go off mission' and step outside the predictable and quantifiable questions set down. They will say it is important to ensure customers are all asked the same questions, making it easier to identify 'hot to drop' prospects and monitor progress to target. And buyers don't escape either, as they too prefer to hard code questions into procurement processes creating scoring tables, i.e., points added and taken away based on supplied answers. And why not? Our brains are largely analytical in makeup so laying out the lines to stay within is what we are 'programmed' to follow. From the rules of business to how we get compensated we like to know what we are doing.

Early in my sales career, I participated in a deal to meet my target for six months. What the customer required, no company could provide, but do you think as salespeople we were going to give up? No way! Every salesperson spent massive amounts of time trying to get their product to deliver the outcome. We all understood it was not possible, but one company agreed to use the product to provide the outcome.

Let me tell you, it did not work, and what transpired next was a lengthy battle between the customer and the supplier. The supplier, in the end, took the product back, which became a massive cost to their business and the salesperson's commission and revenue were reversed. It is not worth it.

I now always ask three questions every time I speak with a customer; is it good for them, Is it good for my company and me? If I cannot answer in the affirmative on all three, I pause and reconsider.

Sean Crichton-Browne, Head of Global Partnerships, MarketCulture Strategies

I was well paid a few years ago to help build a sales tool that scored responses to questions and produced painkiller recommendations. The tool was in effect a hard-coded routine (a spreadsheet was involved) that meant no matter what answer was given, *'boy, did we have the product for you'* was the response. I cringe now at the narrow-mindedness of such an approach, but someone was compensating me at the time so why did I care? And the point was that such tactics were designed to exploit a side of our brains, the converger, that feels comfortable with being given the questions to ask. Why? Firstly, it is easier to scale training if the questions are mapped out in advance, and second, it is less tiring on what is already overcrowded 'real estate' in our heads.

Two brains, one question

Our brain might be a squidgy mess of cells and neurons, but

there is a method in the way we make a decision. Daniel Kahneman suggests it is convenient to think we have two of them - System One and System Two brains, not as two actual physical separated organs, but as two quite distinct response mechanisms to problems and solutions. [100] As we converge on making decisions in a fast, unconscious, and automatic state we are using our System One brain. An effortless *'what you see is what you get'* approach that we use nearly all the time. Our fight or flight reflex. Because we use this brain roughly all the time, but despite what we may think, it is essentially irrational. Yet we will argue that we apply logic and rationale to everything we do. Our System Two brain, however, is used for a tiny proportion of our waking hours where we seek out new or missing information to understand what is happening.

Hormones on fire

When someone asks us a question, our brain relaxes and starts searching for answers and solutions. The 'happy hormone,' dopamine is released, motivating us to seek the correct answer and earn a reward. Or it can go the other way as we fear we might be wrong, causing our hormones to make us behave irrationally at times. This might explain why some people love quizzes and others don't. Or how we react to taking examinations or being asked to explain sales figures that are below par.

When asked a question our brain locks on what we have just heard or read, often causing us to misunderstand the question or rush our answers. Known as <u>instinctive elaboration,</u> we have a reflex that shuts down all other activity while we digest what we have just learned. And as the questions become more complex, we converge our attention onto just one thing at a time, throwing a spanner in the theory of 'multi-tasking.'[101]

For us to push back at our reflexes to anchor on what we think we know and hear we will use a tactic to counter our approach, like a safeguard from being too closed-minded. A tactic that we use to trigger the possibility that anything is possible, and that we thought before, might just be wrong.

Out-of-the-box thinking

Have you heard this one? A young priest asked his bishop, *"may I smoke while praying?"* The answer was an emphatic *"No!"* Later, when he saw an older priest puffing on a cigarette while praying, the younger priest scolded him, *"You shouldn't be smoking while praying! I asked the bishop, and he said I could not do it!"*. *"That is odd,"* the old priest replied, *"because I asked the bishop if I could pray while I'm smoking, and he told me that it was okay to pray at any time!"* [102]

I am sure we all have our own out-of-the-box story we share with others to encourage them to open their minds to new possibilities. But there is a problem with this train of thought. Not because it doesn't work but because it can be used in a lazy fashion that fails to achieve what it sets out to do. In their eagerness to be seen as innovative, agile, and fast, out-of-the-box thinkers will unconsciously 'lead with the answer' thus setting the scene for what happens next. Secondly, the person who is experiencing the problem is often not involved. Instead, proxies will turn up with a confident air of being able to describe the situation facing someone else. And finally, despite the early energy created to find a viable way forward, the pull of getting back to the day job introduces frustration and inertia when interest fades because of work pressures. And because of the fear of running out of steam, the out-of-box euphoria drifts into a sub-plot of closed thinking, eventually shutting down creativity to get a decision.

So how do we stimulate people to not think outside the box but to think there is no box? A way to shake away all their preconceptions and illusions of what they think they know and to give them a completely new place to start. It starts with how we describe the situation we are facing and how we frame our words in an open and non-judgmental way. And one of the best ways to do this is by 'designing beautiful questions.'

It is 3am in Singapore

The words jumped out from the page. It read, *'it is 3am in Singapore. Our colleague has lost service. Describe how you would restore their experience.'* That was it. And in those few words, we were magically transported to Singapore sitting next to the 'colleague' and listening to their problem. A moment that transformed how we thought about asking questions to discover answers. This was new for someone who had stared mindlessly at bid documents with the deluge of largely closed questions, just waiting for a stock answer to be copied and pasted.

The words stimulated a dopamine rush to want to understand more, shaded with vulnerability and intrigue. In those few words, we wanted to know a lot more. For example, who was the colleague, their job, why were they still working at 3am, and why was their experience so affected? Were other people affected, and how much worse could the problem go until resolved? And in fact, what experience were they talking about? How bad could it be? And what was the significance of Singapore? Were there other cities yet to experience this pain? And on and on and on until our curiosity finally got the better of us, and we picked up the phone to speak to *'a colleague in Singapore at 3am'*.

In that one phone call, we got to listen to them explain why they did what they did and how it made them feel when *'service went offline.'* We explored their emotions when this happened, capturing their environment and that of others equally affected by the loss of experience. The call enabled us to stop looking for our usual clues and signals and instead ask, *'what the hell is going on in Singapore at 3am.'*

A beautiful question

Darren Berger describes a beautiful question as *"an ambitious yet actionable question that can begin to shift the way we perceive or think about something - and that might serve as a catalyst to bring about change."* [103] In my mind, the 3am Singapore story has all the hallmarks of a beautiful question. As Convergers we were prepared for System One's run-of-the-mill response only to be disrupted by the beautiful question. And the intriguing thing about the 3am in Singapore story is the person who asked the question. I call her Singapore Woman, but she was the company's Procurement Vice-President. She told me that she was frustrated with the ping-pong nature of doing business with suppliers that follow a well-beaten path of tender responses, frameworks, and governance controls. Her 'beautiful question' was her attempt at disrupting what she felt was a tired and fruitless process that often led to unsatisfactory outcomes no matter who 'won' the bid. Singapore Woman was a Diverger, exercising her System Two brain in the hope it would attract like-minded open diverged people to think differently.

Designing questions

I often use the 3am in Singapore example to encourage people to think about the questions they ask. Our question should be human-centred and focused on the situation, experience or event that is affecting someone else. And secondly, the question should be written in the present tense to encourage the recipient to consider real-world issues happening 'as we speak.' Singapore Woman had cleverly achieved both in her beautiful question. She got us thinking about '3 am in Singapore' making us feel it was happening right now (present) and got us to imagine 'a colleague' (human-centred).

I appreciate in a commercial conversation about problems and solutions it is not possible to dismiss the need for rigour and compliance. But surely there is still a chance to produce a statement that underpins all the business language with a human-centred description as suggested? What stops us? Tradition, processes or a fear of being different?

The right time to ask a silly question

He was a senior leader of a global technology company and had just asked my group of assembled business partners to ask him any question they liked. My arm shot straight up because I had the perfect killer question, or so I thought. He acknowledged my hand and asked me to say a few words before turning to me. He told the group that his door was always open but that the one question he found quite silly was, *'what keeps you awake at night.'* He paused and then pointed to me for my question - which, of course, was the very same question! Oops. He explained that it was a silly question because he always got undisturbed sleep every night. But he did qualify his comment by saying the question was no longer silly if asked to any of his senior leadership team who 'most definitely *do not get a good night's sleep.'*

My stand-out experience didn't work out on that occasion but the question, *'what keeps you awake at night'* is still a keeper for me. Why? In those few words, the question stimulates the other person to think of themselves and what might prevent them from getting a 'good night's sleep.' Framed in the present tense, it creates a mini-drama that encourages them to respond openly and with a level of vulnerability to want to share with you - *'do you know what? I have a real issue with this or that.'* Now I know why I should ask the question - back then I was asking it to be

168

the smart ass in the room!

For me, such examples speak to the importance of thinking about the questions we ask. So what if there was a way to design a better question? A way to demonstrate vulnerability and humility in the discovery that may make all the difference when the pressure to win the game is at its peak.

Not enough time on our hands

If you had sixty minutes to discuss a problem and identify a solution what would you do? According to Albert Einstein, *"if I had an hour to solve a problem, I'd spend 55 minutes thinking about the problem and five minutes thinking about solutions"*.[104] How would you respond to this?

The truth is we view time as a barrier, and we believe we never have enough of it. So when confronted with a problem we unconsciously use our System One brain to analyse what we see and find a solution. We will unconsciously engage our heads, not our hearts or gut. We trust the head to watch the clock and keep us on point. A facet of our cognitive design that we use most of the time is that we use technology as our 'time buddy.' Notifications, alerts, task lists, nudges, alarms - have I missed anything?

So when I say use our Diverger's mindset, I am talking about how we engage our System Two brain, to expose self-awareness, scepticism and vulnerability. And a helpful way to do this is by reframing our questions using a technique called the 5Ws. Five simple questions that when you read them you will say 'yeah I know and always ask them.' Let's see.

What is?

When was the last time in a business meeting did you or anyone else ask, *'are we sure we are solving the right problem here?'* I am sure you are nodding your head that this is your default question, and if so, congratulations. For the head shakers, such a question offers an early chance to frame what happens next. The aid workers in Bangladesh may not have asked this question because they believe they had seen the 'same problem' in Tamil Nadu. And in the case of Singapore woman, she was deliberately not answering the question by framing her requirement to encourage us to ask it instead.

Who has?

Too often business leaders will describe the problem in minute detail but become too generalised when asked to describe the experience of the person with the problem. They will loosely tag someone on their mind, but when pushed to describe the 'empathy map' of this person, they become defensive and try to close down the discussion to move on. I call it the people like me fallacy, where shortcuts encourage us to make assumptions about someone else's situation - all because we think we have a shared experience.

For decades, the automotive and insurance industry has relied on crash test dummies to improve the design of their products to make them safer for people to use. Except that throughout this time the assumption they knew 'who had the problem' was biased towards men. Why? Because the crash test dummy was built to the dimensions of the 'average male.' A factor that led to women being more likely to be seriously hurt in an accident than men because of misalignment of airbags, side door protection and seat belt configuration.[105] An entire industry convinced they knew 'who has' but had been blindsided by bias and a converged mindset.

It is examples like this that underline that these two pieces of information - what is the problem and who is affected most are the most misunderstood questions asked in business every day. It is sobering to consider that no amount of cool technology will help fix what happens next if these two questions are not fully understood by all concerned.

As Convergers it is instinctive to want to solve problems even when we don't have all the information to hand in. The old age adage that 'the sooner we start the sooner we finish.' Relying on cognitive shortcuts to latch onto incomplete information or previously held views to speed us along.

What if?

When James Dyson took his vacuum cleaner out onto his garden lawn to explore why the dust collection was not working satisfactorily, he was exercising the What If question. His innovation story led to the buzz phrase, 'doing a Dyson,' and no wonder. Dyson wasn't thinking outside the box, he was thinking there was no box! He had previously observed an industrial sawmill using a 'cyclonic separator' to remove dust from the air, which led him to challenge, *'what if there was no bag.'* He would say, *"I thought the same principle of separation might work on a vacuum cleaner. I rigged up a quick prototype, and it did."* [106] The rest is history.

When queues were too long in their theme parks, Disney asked themselves, *'how might we improve guest experiences'* which led them to ask, *'what if people didn't need to queue?'* An inquisitive human-centred approach led to the innovation known as Magic Band, an all-in access device to everything for their guests. [107]

When people ask a question, our brain transparently looks in our cognitive bookmarks for previous information, data, or experiences of similar situations. All done in superfast mode, so quick we don't know we are doing it. But when we ask a 'What If' question something different happens. The first thing is that our brain turns on our Diverger's radar. Now our brain stops looking for previously held information and urges us to go below the surface of what we are hearing. A question that asks, *'what if anything were possible,'* and considers even the craziest idea might be possible without judgement or criticism from those around us.

Since 2018 I have been working in an advisory capacity with a 260-year-old social improvement organisation trying to digitally connect its members. Some false starts in the past had left them under-confident. Despite the demand for better online services and low satisfaction scores, the initiative lacked momentum. I tried to understand the blockers. Here are just a few I discovered; it was not considered a priority even though it was recognised as important, the team could not see the potential for what it might add to the organisation's impact, and they lacked the skills to effectively implement a solution, and of course, they were too busy.

I could see a bigger push was required to inspire action. I mobilised a team of thought and practice leaders to function as visionaries and benevolent provocateurs. We created scenarios for how the organisation could use digital technology to improve the member experience and drive positive social impact. The themes included a virtual coffee house, a member matching service, and a self-organising platform. We promoted the event with a visual social media campaign featuring the leaders and their scenarios. We invited digitally savvy members to join the participatory design event, where we ran design workshops for each theme. We were able to collectively imagine 'how might we' scenarios that delivered value to the community. Members enthusiastically joined the movement, and we finally gained momentum and funding.

The secret was mobilising an engaged group of stakeholders to be part of the co-design process from the very start. This was the approach that was subsequently taken forward.

Ann Longley, Director, Something New Together

Think back to situations where you have been sitting there listening to people explaining their problems. Were there moments perhaps because of time constraints that you didn't grasp fully answers to 'What Is' and 'Who Has'? Be honest and think whether you and others were guilty of sidestepping curiosity to experiment with 'What If' to get to the 'What Wows' and 'What Works' sides of the conversation.

It might well be that the CEO in my Madrid story was ' guilty' of merging these questions into her single problem statement - *'we don't have enough pipeline.'* She was also telling us who had the problem - we did. And was sublimely telling us 'what works' - find the missing number, which introspectively would have been the answer to the 'what wows' question. But what was missing was the 'what if' question. Of course, this is my interpretation of that day. The CEO was fearful of asking us to consider 'what if' because of an inherent feeling of uncertainty. Asking a room of highly paid intelligent people to stop converging and start diverging might have been an amazing experience but would it have worked? Would chaos ensue and how would she control the outcome? Much easier therefore to announce the problem and the expected result and let them go.

What wows?

I can still recall the moment when I lifted the lid on my first iPhone box, The imperceptible 'whoosh' as the lid came off still sticks in my mind. I am told it is a 'seven-second' experience. And I don't think I am alone. A wow moment that Apple knew would occur and which explains why so many of their customers still keep the boxes. [108]

But what is 'wow'? People will often say to each other *'we need the Wow factor"* just before embarking on a conversation about innovation. They say this because they believe they need unique and ground-breaking ideas to solve their problems by exciting customers. They feel that if they don't have 'wow' then they will fall short and not succeed. Something that is different and that no one else has considered before. Something that will fire up the happy hormones to get people excited and on board. Something their unconscious self is thinking about the Apple whoosh.

Go back again to your innovative idea. Where is the 'wow'? Could you describe it to someone else? Does it still excite your happy hormones or has that time been and gone and you hang on to it because of loyalty or because you are still paying for it? Are you a secret iPhone box hoarder?

I remember a chat with a 'triage bot' discussing an overdue unpaid bill. My hopes were not high, but it seemed impossible to get through to a human being, so I persevered. To my surprise, during the conversation, I found out I would be getting a refund not a red warning. I did not expect this at all especially given I was talking to a line of code. My true wow experience of recent times. A human will have designed their algorithm to combine a level of human behaviour and sentiment with a business process. DBOFO tick in the box!

What works?

When John F Kennedy said the immortal words, "*I believe that this nation should commit itself to achieve the goal [..] of landing a man on the Moon and returning him safely to Earth,*" he was describing a problem statement with a significant Wow moment.[109] His backdrop was the East versus West superpower struggle, which formed his <u>what is the problem</u> question. America was falling behind the USSR in space travel, and JFK wanted to push back. He made the <u>who has the problem</u> everyone's problem, like a shared pain. He then posed the <u>what if</u> question by asking people to imagine a fellow American landing on the moon and returning safely to earth. No doubt, an incredible horizon for people to digest at that time. The <u>wow</u> moment came with a timeframe that they would return a fellow American safely to earth within the decade. Through his challenging and inquiring speech, he set off a train of thought that, seven years later, saw Neil Armstrong take those first steps on the moon. The <u>what works</u> question. JFK had used the five Ws. His inquisitive statement reached into the System Two brains of the NASA engineers and the broader American population that got them to think - 'there was no box.'

When we converge, we unconsciously compress the five W questions in an attempt to solve the problem and move on i.e., sellers will group retailers with the same issue with stock inventory and buyers will sign off solutions that competitors are using. And where it tends to go wrong is when we make assumptions about 'What is the problem' and 'Who has the problem.' From that point on our attempts to find solutions can go disastrously wrong and all because we didn't spend enough time challenging our assumptions. When we diverge, however, we are on high alert to experiment with the questions we ask and start again. We do this without fear of failure or ridicule encouraging others to prototype and test are known facts, assumptions, and biases. For example, the ACME example earlier might benefit from a period of observing a customer using the website and speaking with them about how it made them feel. Through observation, we might discover a better way to solve the problem our boss gave us. And one of the most overlooked aspects of our ability to understand each other better is how we use (or don't) the 'two eyes, one mouth' skill. As John Le Carré, spy author wrote in his famous novel Tinker Tailor Solider Spy, *"a desk is a dangerous place to watch the world."*[110]

Why is that happening?

The driver stopped the streetcar and climbed out of the warm cab to clear off the snow covering the window. Sitting inside, Mary Anderson watched with eyes wide open while her fellow passengers looked on in frustration at the further delay to their journey. It was 1902 and led to the birth of what we now know as the windscreen wiper. [111]

Mary Anderson asked herself a series of 'how might we' and 'what if' questions as she sat in the shoes of fellow passengers. I can imagine Mary was asking herself, *'how might we make the trams run to schedule'* and *'what if we could clear the snow without stopping the tram.'* Sadly, Mary did not get any money for her Windows Device

Cleaning invention, but in 2011 she was inducted into the Inventors Hall of Fame. Mary Anderson was not a behavioural scientist or engineer. She was a realtor. But in my mind, Mary Anderson was an out-and-out Diverger, in a tram car full of Convergers.

When we diverge, we activate our senses to help us improve at noticing things. And the power of watching other people is an often-forgotten attribute we can all rediscover if only we lifted our heads above the screen, right? We may all ask ourselves whether the digital world is corroding this most natural human characteristic we were so good at when younger. The packed commuter train or business shuttle flight is usually quiet except for mouse clicks and keyboard taps. At festivals and sporting events, we can't even clap anymore because we are holding our smartphones. Have we become so bad at observing what is happening before us that we miss the obvious? Like the occasional gorilla perhaps?

Researchers showed participants a video of people playing basketball and asked them to count the number of passes between the players. Then after a few seconds, a gorilla walked across the screen. Despite the obvious, many participants failed to see the gorilla, who was a woman wearing a costume. This is known as 'inattentional blindness' - a trait we all suffer from at one time or another. And in a high-speed digital world, we will miss more gorillas.

Spin that roulette wheel

I am just so unlucky when I gamble. I never seem to win,

but there is always the next time, right? The design of modern technology is a bit like gambling. The designers create an experience that, in many cases, mimics the roulette wheel, encouraging us to spin again to see if we have a reward. I mean that unconscious pull down for your finger on your social media feeds to check if there is anything new for you. And even though we might not get anything, we will keep on 'spinning that wheel,' making us feel guilty to stop. And then think about the dynamics of a casino or amusement arcade. What is the common denominator apart from the money being won or lost? Noise. All those beeps, buzzes, and rumbles trigger our happy hormones to spend more. It is the same with our technology today. Whether it is notifications on our phones that someone is outside our house, social media nudges or the gamification of corporate learning, we are being bombarded from all angles.

And even when we turn off 'tech,' our brains are still tuned into listening for those nudges, reducing our focus on what we believe we are giving our full attention to.[112] It is no surprise, therefore, that we don't see the gorilla. Even though this research was conducted twenty years ago, I think it might be easier now to influence our attention (or not).

Behaviour

If you live in Dubai and like the IKEA brand you might easily rely on home delivery as your preference. Why drive a long distance when you can enjoy the convenience of at-door service? So the IKEA store in Dubai tried something to see if they could change consumer behaviour to physically come into the store. Called the 'buy with your time' incentive, customers could earn credit based on the distance they travelled to the store. At checkout, shoppers would show the cashier their Google Maps timeline, which records their past trips. The cashier would then convert their purchases into 'time currency' prices. [113] A five-minute travel time equalled a veggie hot dog, for example.

What IKEA was doing was experimenting with consumer behaviour. Nothing particularly unique in this, of course. We see the retail and entertainment industry, in particular, doing this all the time as they sound out the marketplace with nudges. And we have seen it recently in healthcare settings during the 2020 pandemic, i.e., stickers for social distancing and songs for handwashing, to encourage us to develop habits that would alter our behaviour.

Habits

Research published by the European Journal of Social Psychology suggests it takes 18 to 254 days for a person to form a new habit.[114] There are times when we find a new behaviour relatively easy to pick up and form a habit, while others seem to cause us pain and heartache. And what about the bad habits, we develop without realising? Do we develop them much easier than good ones? Why is that? And then, in the context of the business world, how good are we at changing behaviours ethically and sustainably?

Research from Stanford professor, BJ Fogg, suggests there are three behavioural traits that we need to display simultaneously to change our behaviour - motivation, ability, and prompt.

Fogg even has it written down as an algorithm.

B (behaviour) = M (motivation) + A (ability) + P (prompt)

Try and pop your innovative thing into the above sum. Can you easily identify your motivation, ability and prompt? Do you concur that at times the simultaneous aspect is a challenge? We might love the innovation of a sports watch that helps us stay healthier, but if we are working in a strange city we might not feel comfortable exercising so much.

There is a lovely story about executives at a well-known car manufacturer who asked employees to think freely about *'ways to increase productivity'* only to receive blank stares. When they reframed the question as *'how might we find ways to make your jobs easier,'* they could barely keep up with the number of innovative suggestions. As Fogg says, *"Goals are harmful unless they guide you to make specific behaviours easier. Do not focus your motivation on doing Behaviour X; instead, focus on making Behaviour X easier to do."* [115] Consider Fogg's words - *'make specific behaviours easier.'* How often have we wrestled with a problem or an opportunity to get a resolution that on reflection has just made everything the times harder for the person we were trying to help? Remember it is in our cognitive design to always look for ways to make our lives easier - never harder. Unless we are trying to join the SAS or run a marathon!

What is the motivation?

Think about something recently that has changed in your behaviour and the motivation behind your decisions. You might have initiated it yourself, i.e., losing weight, learning to cook Thai food, or authoring a book. Or it might have been imposed on you due to a change of circumstances, i.e., a new process at work, a rise in tax contributions, or a health scare. But is motivation enough? Naturally, we lean into anything that motivates us for the better, making us believe it is helping us be safer and happier. The developer community works hard to make their sites and apps attractive to us, making it harder for us to step away. Yet, in a business context, we have to ask ourselves whether motivation is enough to change the behaviour of someone with a problem or need. Even if that happens, does it help or is it just a quick fix? Just because the CEO tells us we have to make a change doesn't automatically flow into behavioural change. And don't get me started on parenting and behavioural change.

What about ability?

It is one thing to say you have the motivation to change your behaviour, but what if you don't have the tools? Not just the tangible resources, like cash, facilities, and time, but also the intangibles - like health, skills, and confidence. Often this perceived (or real) lack of ability will cloud our judgement and can derail any plans we have no matter what the motivation is.

And what about the mindset of those around you? Do the

people we work with influence our ability to change behaviour? How will that impact our ability if everyone else appears to be making changes with joyful abandon while we struggle privately? Or is the design of a digital tool contrary to our way of understanding its use, creating frustration and stress, and reducing our ability to make progress? I say this when I look at the design of everyday things that are heavily digitised now, often out of reach of people without the cognitive ability to use them.

To highlight my point is the ever-increasing trend towards digitised car parks, where cash is no longer an option to park your car. Why? I can see owners and managers of such facilities being able to collect revenues without having to physically empty cash boxes. And for us, being able to pay for parking without needing coins is a godsend when in a rush. In terms of DBOFO, this is all good, and positive outcomes are present. Except not for those who distrust sharing payment details over the phone or have the ability to be online to use apps and websites.

What is the prompt?

And even if there is sufficient motivation and ability in place, it may still not be enough to reach the mountain top of sustainable growth. The rebirth of the QR (quick response) code as a measure for access control to public spaces during a pandemic, for example. Yet the QR code has been around for decades and never really changed anyone's behaviour at scale before now. Did it need the prompt of a health crisis to help change people's behaviour? Had Fogg's equation suddenly landed simultaneously into the laps of the hospitability sector to influence consumer behaviour? Will we now see QR codes in restaurants and bars as a valid alternative to having our orders taken down by a human being?

Identifying the prompt is the most challenging aspect of the behavioural change discussion because it is a fluid factor that can often be outside our influence and driven by external forces we can't control or fully understand. And this is the most exciting aspect of an inquiring mind that many in business could do well to not forget.

My 12-year-old son is on the autistic spectrum. He really struggles to cope with secondary school. The school are fantastic, but we need to help him see things differently. A renowned clinical psychologist I know suggested we look at Jane McGonigal's work and her book 'Superbetter.' [116] My son loves gaming and would happily spend all his waking hours playing on his computer. What is "Superbetter"? It is a framework that activates the psychological strengths of gameplay to build resilience and success in real life.

This approach strives to promote levels of personal growth due to stress and change. Improving protective factors like optimism and reducing obstacles to resilience, such as anxiety. The gem for my son and me is the quests the book contains. These quests are designed to help with mindset, emotional and social control, and other key psychological strengths such as optimism. I have used his love of gaming to show him of what he is capable. He is now willing to challenge himself and strive to improve at his driving games, push his boundaries and get a better and better lap time. These quests look to tap into this and apply it to other scenarios in his life, like secondary school.

Has it worked for my son? My son does not go to school with a smile on his face yet. But this is a lifelong journey, and success is not black and white. He is certainly using the lessons from the book in his game, and I have seen snippets of him applying these to other scenarios he finds difficult. I will certainly preserve and work through more quests with my son to try and help him cope with the pressures of life.
Doug Field, Joint CEO, East Anglia Co-Operative Society

Free Guy takes the Fogg test

He had plenty of motivation. His industry was on a trajectory to digitisation driven by legislation, competitiveness, and skills. He also had the ability. He had the money for a start and support systems to receive the new technology with resources lined up to onboard and stabilise. And he had the prompt. His customers were increasingly turning to outcomes-based thinking for construction projects that offered greater financial rewards and more predictable order book status. Three ticks. Or was it? What if we turned it around and thought about the people working for him? What was their motivation, ability, and prompt? Had we overlooked this in our response, and had his people fallen into the same trap when they prepared the bid? If I were to go back in time, I would have challenged Free Guy on his understanding of the behavioural algorithm, not for his purposes but for the people who worked for his company.

Crisis of prioritisation

Let me ask you. Do you think in business, particularly there is a crisis of prioritisation on a level not witnessed before? Or has the digital world helped us make sense of what is important and what is not? Where do you sit on this? And in our personal lives has the 'list of things to do' gotten longer and more complicated often because of events outside our control? Or does that depend on our age and social situation.? No straight answer - how could there be but the one thing I have heard many business leaders echo is *we just don't know where to* start.'

I recall a meeting over coffee with a senior business leader that had the hallmarks of such a challenge. The conversation was one about customer satisfaction and the role of technology to optimise what his customers thought of his service delivery organisation. My 'agenda' was to sell him something (obviously), but I was intrigued to see what his view of the crisis of prioritisation was. Did he have one or was he on top of it all?

In the chat, we got to talk about how his leadership team bought innovations to his desk. He did admit that he was faced with increasing demands from his customer base and financial prudence from up high. A balancing act not made easier by the firehose of innovative ideas from his leadership team, eager to 'be the one.' He complained that his people sometimes found it harder to think 'human.' Had they lost the ability to inquire, or were they just too busy to reach out? So I scribbled down the Fogg algorithm on a napkin and briefly explained the context. When we finished he took the napkin away with him and promised to give me feedback the next time we met. We spoke again months later, and he told me he was now using the Fogg model as a 'priority triage' with his leadership team. Not to replace proper due diligence, but to get a gut reaction sense check of ideas coming down the line. A tactic that gave him a moment of pause to recalibrate. Having used it for a few weeks, he had seen encouraging signs that his people were now thinking 'better' about the intended behaviours their innovations were hoping to improve.

He accepted the Fogg test was just a tactic, but given his crisis of prioritisation, it was refreshing to keep his people on their toes! And in fairness isn't that what business is all about anyway? Tactics to survive the next crisis?

Hint

Take the Fogg triage test on the priorities on your mind. It might be your list of things to do at home or a business prioritisation matrix for the next quarter. Start by asking yourself *'am I confident that I and others can describe the behavioural change in the person who I am trying to help when I complete this task?'* Then write a single sentence to explain the intended behavioural change i.e., *'the children will be able to make their breakfast and tidy up afterwards.* Do it in silence and compare notes with other members of your team or family. And if you can pass that confidence test, then ask yourself, *'what would be the motivation for all concerned to make this work?'* Then followed by, *'do we have the ability to give this our best shot,'* and finally ask, *'can I identify the prompt that will make the behaviour sustainable.'* Perhaps the children's breakfast idea is a tough one! But I hope you get the drift.

If you answer any of the behavioural traits with reasonable doubt, go back to the start and examine your assigned priority i.e., maybe asking your children to prepare their breakfast is not the priority you first thought, but getting them out of bed first is. Could you now reframe the problem to see if you could find a more successful way to change behaviour?

This exercise can be an entertaining use of your time to reflect on the priorities that consume your everyday world, helping you reframe how you might see things as important versus nice to have. I call it a triage because that is what it is trying to do. In the busyness of everyday life having a mental conscious thought to help frame what you are looking at might be just enough to question motives, concepts, and priorities. This is not a panacea but merely a tactic to disrupt how clear you and others understand the priorities in need of resolution.

And when there is money involved to spend wisely having a simple framework to help show others how to rationalise their 'cool ideas' can be a great tool to have at your disposal.

Status quo bias

To change our behaviour we have to be much more

inquisitive about the other person's motivations, abilities, and prompts. The way we design systems nowadays is heavily slanted towards behavioural change. The technology industry like others invests heavily in the science of behavioural change. They are veritable factories of human-centric design and behavioural analysis. But they can only do so much, and they also suffer from bias and illusion. After all whilst they try to understand their customers better they are also in the business of winning the game.

There is an old English proverb *'a change is as good as a rest'* that suggests changing something is just as good as doing nothing. Sound familiar?

Stop Start Better

Every time we wake up, go to work or have lunch, we change our perspectives and experiences. The same can be said for our businesses. They open up, they operate, and they close down; inevitable change events over which we have some control over the inputs and outputs. But growth?

Strategy is about what you are planning to do but often not what you are going to stop doing. Michael E Porter even suggested, *"strategy requires you to make trade-offs in competing - to choose what not to do."* [117] We do this because it is stimulating and positive to talk about plans, avoiding the more negative side, where we no longer want to be focusing our time. Except that often, the things we said we would stop doing have just kept on going.

Hint

Run your <u>Stop Start Better</u> analysis. Think about the last 12 months and consider just one thing you have committed to STOP doing. Ask yourself whether you have actually stopped doing that thing or if it still lingers for one reason or another. It could be that you committed to stop using social media, stop cluttering your wardrobes or dispense with a fruitless process at work. Then think about one thing you have committed to START doing. Have you started doing this thing, or find you are still talking about it instead? You were going to listen to podcasts while on the train, visit local museums at weekends or have a weekly 121 call with colleagues from another office. Now think about something you are doing BETTER today than you were twelve months ago. You might find that you have become better at letting others speak in meetings, or your sleep has improved due to a change you initiated in your lifestyle. Reflect on your responses and why they are what they are. If you find that they have not been as successful as hoped, consider the barriers, and prompts that led to your discovery. Did you misunderstand the level of resistance from yourself and others and could you look at the Fogg algorithm to identify where it might be lacking? i.e., motivation and promptness were good but after three months the money ran out.

The <u>Stop Start Better</u> technique is a chance for people to be honest and open about their track record for stopping old ways, starting new ones, and executing better than before. And what is interesting about this technique is that it can apply to businesses as well. Imagine asking the CEO the same question. How good is our company at stopping what it says it will stop, starting what it says it will start and getting better at things it said it would get better at? This a question they may not have been asked before (remember the silly question angle) but I wager a bet that the CEO would find the answer quite a challenge but in a good way.

The Diverger's toolbox

The power of inquiry is the most valuable tool in Diverger's toolbox. It is about being more curious, more inquisitive, and more vulnerable to making a deeper connection with the other person in the conversation. When we do show our inquisitive side we develop a stronger level of trust. People will naturally share their situation much more easily than if you appear to be only interested in your position. Remember the self-orientation aspect of the Trust Equation? If we spend too long talking about 'us,' we will lower our trustworthiness with the other person. Do we train sales to think like this? Can we help them be more trustworthy whilst still finding the missing bullet holes?

Of all the amazing sellers I have worked with the one stands out attribute they had, was their ability to get to know as much as they could about the other person's situation. They will admit I am sure they didn't get professionally trained or one-to-one coaching. They would say it was down to experience and some luck, but I like to think they were using their inbuilt curiosity gene and open mindset to listen more than they talked. A skill that is a lot harder than it might seem.

I have covered so far how we try to understand problems better and how to use our curiosity and inquiry to ask 'beautiful' questions. All tactics help uncover the problem and the people involved but even when we do all this we can stand or fall on how we communicate our values. This leads me to the next chapter about how we can 'think' stories. In the words of Lisa Cron, *"Story, as it turns out, was crucial to our evolution - more so than opposable thumbs. Opposable thumbs let us hang on; story told us what to hang on to."*[118]

CHAPTER 7

THINK BETTER STORIES

"After nourishment, shelter and companionship, stories are what we need most in the world."
- PHILIP PULMAN

Forget Wall Street, La Rambla or the Champs - Élysées. The street you should take a stroll down is Dollar Street. When you do you will meet the Santos Carneiro and Gigana Dan families. You will see how they prepare food, where they sleep, how they entertain themselves, deal with personal hygiene and what their aspirations are for a better life. The Dan family treasure photos of the children and dream of buying a new house, while the Carneiro family love their laptop and want to buy a new microwave.

And the fascinating thing about Dollar Street and these families is that the Santos Carneiros family live in Brazil and the Dans family live in Serbia. You see Dollar Street is a virtual street. A street flattened by technology to share stories through video and photos that put us all on the same street.

Dollar Street is a storytelling platform created by Anna Rosling Rönnlund, who wanted to visualise how we all live on the same street with incomes available to us. Anna explains, *"People in other cultures are often portrayed as scary or exotic. This has to change. We want to show how people live. It seemed natural to use photos as data so people can see for themselves what life looks like at different income levels. Dollar Street lets you visit many homes all over the world. Without travelling."* [119]

Ticks the box

I like Dollar Street because in my mind it ticks all the boxes of a good story. It has protagonists - the families of Santos Carneiro and Gigana Dan and many more. Dollar Street makes a human connection through the stories it shares. The photos and videos encourage the viewer to ask, *'how does that compare to how we live our lives.'* I share the Dollar Street example, not because it is unique, but because it isn't Facebook or the other mainstream social platforms that share stories too. Dollar Street is the metaphor in my mind for how businesses can succeed by telling their stories through the power of visualisation.

In business, we see plenty of visualised comparisons and contrasts. Our social media and TV screens are awash with businesses trying the most creative ways to present their story to us. The Christmas adverts that became infectious across UK screens stick in my mind, telling human-centred stories though perhaps not based on the original plot and characters! Like the 'man on the moon' advert that touched many a heart when it first hit our screens during Christmas time.[120]

Where has the drama gone

In the seconds that it takes for you to read what comes next, your senses will be bombarded with millions of pieces of information. Your conscious mind, however, has only enough capacity to process tiny amounts of data simultaneously. Not that impressive but it boils down to survival. I can tell you that the weather is sunny today, and your unconscious mind will note it and flag it as likely irrelevant. But to tell you that today's weather is a red warning of danger to life, you will almost certainly pay attention.

Stories allow us to simulate experiences as if caught up in the drama. In the Stone Age, this was akin to waiting when you hear the 'rustling of the bushes' versus running as fast as you can as a lion emerges for its lunch. Hopefully, our stories are less life and death but still retain that feeling of 'stick or twist.,' i.e., If you believe my innovative idea, you are likelier to twist, but if my story doesn't arouse your hormones then you will hit the status quo button. Or do what Free Guy did and not sign the contract.

When we hear a story we unconsciously look for cues; what is the drama happening right now and who is the protagonist involved? We do this because we want to be drawn into the ups and downs of what comes next and how it stimulates our thoughts. From an early age, we grew up with the classic 'once upon a time' rags to riches and good versus evil tales that emerged from books. We would go to the cinema and theatre to submerge our imaginations in drama and heroism. We think in stories. Always have and always will. It is hardwired into our brains to constantly look for meaning, pulling out what might be a threat and how it might affect us.

The dangers of narrative

But for business audiences familiar with the issues on their mind, stories take on a quite different perspective. People turn on their *'what's in it for me'* radar relying on gut instinct to vote for or against someone's pitch. And for the people pitching the narrative, will complain that it is hard to build drama into their stories because they aren't the creator of the content. This often means they don't believe the story or are only 'trained' to talk about the plot and not the human-centric nature of why their pitch is so relevant to their listener.

What is a story anyway?

It's recognised that a story needs a plot; something that stimulates the question of 'what is happening right now.' Then it needs some drama, a suggestion of something that has changed. Then it needs a protagonist who is affected by the drama. Someone we can connect with and think about our plight.

Then the story needs to <u>ask a question</u> of its audience that teases a thought of *'what's at stake'* for the protagonist if their situation doesn't improve? And finally, what is the protagonist going to be able to do to <u>change their situation</u> or who is going to be the hero to help them?

The plot in the 3am Singapore story was *'someone was having difficulty at 3 am with a system issue'*. The protagonist was *'a colleague.'* And the question being asked was how would *'their experience be restored'*. And the change? Well, that was for the person reading the story, the potential supplier to develop a desirable, feasible, viable solution and be the hero. All laid out in less than twenty words. I have seen bid documents running into hundreds of pages that fail to tell any semblance of a story in this way.

Happy hormone time

A good story activates parts of the brain that connects the listener to the ideas the storyteller is sharing. This is known as neural coupling. A good story has to allow the other person to say to themselves, *'how am I going to feel at the end.'* And to do this, we need to excite the happy hormone - a chemical reaction in our brains that releases dopamine when we hear or see something that excites and provokes us.

But when I look back on my technology days, the sales playbook was less about human emotions and more about technical prowess. We would use the jealousy factor heavily - *'your competitors are signing up to us in droves.'*

An approach biased towards us and not the person receiving the story. Our stories would be heavily plot-centric, not human-centric. The Year 2000 computer bug storyline is a historic example of this, that spoke of 'aeroplanes falling out of the skies' and 'crashed banking systems'. Little is said, however, about people directly. It was much easier to tell stories that felt 'strong' and 'absolute.' It also meant the stories could be told to groups of people with similar issues which played right into the hands of Convergers playing the finite game. If more people are the same then the story can be mass-produced and measured a lot easier than tailored personal narratives that lack scale.

Stories tire us out

We tell our children bedtime stories to help develop their vocabulary, engagement, and conversation. Of course, that is a huge part of it, but when they are quite little telling them a story also tires them out. Those soft-spoken tales (from grandparents often) are entirely made up but stimulate the little one to close their eyes and slip into a deep sleep.

And this tiring effect can also carry through to adult life when confronted with someone telling a story. Imagine that you are on the stage just about to present your beautifully crafted presentation to an expectant audience. You might be first up or lucked out and got the last slot before the bar or home time. Either way, you are confident because your slides and narrative are exactly what people want to hear. And in your presentation, you have cleverly mixed videos, images and hard-hitting bullet points all necessary to lay out your point of view. Now imagine you are one of the audience. What are they thinking? Or is too late because you are already rockin' and rollin' through your presentation? Perhaps you move about the stage waving your hands to illustrate individual points or stand firm behind the podium.

Stories are stressful

And don't forget the influence of stress. Not yours because that is often a given when giving a presentation, but theirs. Stress increases the hormone release of oxytocin that disrupts the ability to think rationally. Keep this in mind as you think about your story. Do you ever consider that your story might be falling foul of the 'need to know' rule? A situation where the storyteller over-indulgences the audience with more information than they need to know, inadvertently confusing them and causing them stress with their attention span.

And at this point, I have to mention ' bullet points.' We have all done this. Built a slide deck or document that we feel needs more emphasis so we 'add more bullet points.' It is as if the original page full wasn't enough. We need more. I've been guilty of bullet point overdose. Just consider how hard someone's brain has to work to read all your painstakingly crafted bullet points on the screen. And then the extra effort to connect what you are saying with the animation effects going on over your shoulder. Imagine the effort necessary for their brain to filter out what is essential or not to them whilst soaking in your verbal communication simultaneously.

Like a flock of birds

When one bird flaps its wings, the flock responds as they soar into the sky as one unit. An incredible sight to see on an early morning. Similarly, when one person tells a story, it isn't long before others 'flap their wings' to follow them and amplify the story to others. It is what we have been doing as a species since Adam and Eve and with social media, as the current transport mechanism for many, it is now relentless. And in business, all it takes is one person to 'flap their wings' with a good story before an entire flock rises beside them. Now think about your stories. Are you going to share with them something they can flap their wings over and influence others to follow suit? When is your 'killer moment' going to come in your slide deck to see them fly away with vigour and your message?

The case study dilemma

In the words of Simon Sinek, *"People do not buy what you do; they buy why you do it."*[121] Yet the case study - that vital piece of sales currency - often fails to expose the Why sufficiently for the audience. Perhaps this is unfair? But what is the purpose of the case study? In my mind, a case study is a 'device' that is commonly used in the sales conversation to amplify one's capability and relevance to complete a quite specific function, aimed at giving reassurance to a prospective customer. We rely on them to build up trustworthiness with others by making them feel we have their best interests at heart, that we can understand their problem and have the right credentials to help them. And why not? It is unlikely any of us would entertain giving a plastering job to someone who can't describe previous work completed for satisfied customers.

But the problem with case studies is that they are often plot based. Consider this, *'Company X had a problem with health and safety accident reporting at their European sites and solved it by implementing solution Y which in turn enabled them to commence a new business stream Z.'* Over simplistic I admit but where is the drama? Where are the characters? Who changed their behaviour as a result of solution Y and could comment on how it made them move on to working on business stream Z? No doubt factual and evidence-based but wouldn't this story make a better connection if there were a blend of plot and character-based narratives? Perhaps it was just one individual or hundreds of thousands of them?

Time and place

Imagine you have won a piece of work and before you start doing anything else, the first thing you do is to write the case study - as if you have FINISHED the work. Why? Our emotions fire up positively at the inception of a new piece of work. Adrenalin is flowing at the thought of doing something new that is wanted by others around us. And for them, they are also pumped up because a problem they have will be soon fixed. You know that feeling you get when shaking the hand of the designer that your dream home is on its way. But how do we often feel at the end of the job? Have our experiences become jaded or compromised by what happened? We may have hit difficulties and conflicts that change our emotions.

The forward-thinking case study is a chance to put down the results and outcomes you expect to see as if they have just happened. A story that describes what the problem was solved (drama), who gained the most benefit (protagonist), how it all worked and what was the 'wow' (outcome). A narrative that can be put away and retrieved for comparison when the work is completed and to give colour to how case studies can become stories, not just words on paper. After all, why wait until the end of a piece of work? Surely if there is clarity of mission and everyone is on the 'same page' writing the case study at the start makes no difference. The sentiments and outcomes should be the same, right? And the power of doing a forward-thinking case study is not just to have words on paper that get filed away. I have used forward-thinking case studies on three occasions - twice successful, once not. On each successful experience, teams' discovered something that helped them re-frame the programme before they started. And the time it was less successful was because we collectively found that the scope and vision of the case study were a long way off what others thought it should be. The net result was the project never started, saving money and time to do something more important. There is a lesson in here somewhere.

What's the hook

"Where's Papa going with that axe said Fern to her mother as they were setting the table for breakfast. Out to the

doghouse, replied Ms Arable. Some pigs were born last night. I do not see why he needs an axe, continued Fern, who was only eight." [122]

The first sentence of this story, from the children's book Charlotte's Web, is intoxicating. Nothing focuses the mind as much as drama and uncertainty, and for millions of children, this opening statement sets hormones racing. In a short few words, the author introduces suspense mixed in with a child's wide-eyed curiosity and innocence. The drama surrounding papa and the axe leads us to anticipate what will happen next. What happens to the pigs? What did papa need with an axe, anyway? What was for breakfast?

We need a narrative. A progression of events starts with an opening scene depicting the problem confronting the main character. Followed by a description of rising action as peril or loss unravels. Then a climax where the problem resolves as the main character is saved by the hero. But in a business where we believe we know the plot and have solutions in mind our stories meander without a clear and impactful explanation. When we hear cries for 'narrative' we can believe we have one in the oven - when we most likely don't. Nassim Nicholas Taleb says, *"the narrative fallacy addresses our limited ability to look at sequences of facts without weaving an explanation into them. Explanations bind facts together. They make them all the more easily remembered; they help them make more sense."* [123]

When we hear a story we look to the author for a sign that something is about to change - and not always for the better. The little girl in Charlotte's Web is drawn into her curiosity about what *'papa is doing,'* regardless of whether it will end well for the pigs or not.

And there must be a consequence of your story that you think about as you write your words. If we leave this to our audience to decide for themselves then we shouldn't be surprised if they don't behave as we want them to. Or, as I heard the other day, *'Act I is you explaining how you got someone up into a tree, Act 2 is you throwing stones at them, and Act 3 is how you got them back down from the tree - safely.'*

Am I tuned in?

He was a young software developer eager to get an appointment with me. I had enough time to see him before rushing to catch a flight home to the UK. I outlined my problem statement to him, a technical issue I needed fixing. I thought it odd he did not make notes or tap away at his tablet, but each to their own. We parted with a commitment from him that he would be in touch. I took this to mean I would receive a sales proposal a few days later. A document would take several pages to turn before finding anything to do with you and your problem - fluff masquerading as a story.

But this young man was different. Two hours later to my great surprise I heard from him again. Up popped an email on my Blackberry (yes, I had one of those). He returned to his office, grabbed a video camera, and filmed himself visualising my story on his whiteboard. I sat in the taxi, watching him describe his story to help me. A story that blew me away. I called him right back and gave him a verbal order for the work. A response that was out of character for me, breaking a corporate due diligence rule somewhere, but no doubt the result of an onslaught of happy hormones from watching his video story.

When we spoke again I asked him about his approach. His answer was wonderfully simple yet powerful. He said he had one shot at winning me over and that I would be travelling immediately after the meeting. He explained that he had spotted a small window to excite me and observed my preference for drawing my issue on the whiteboard. He assumed (correctly) that I had a preference for visual cues. He also knew if he let time elapse, my memory of the meeting would have faded. This guy, who I will call Thinking Guy, had done his homework on me!

Be a story thinker

Thinking Guy was not only a first-class storyteller but a story thinker too. First, he put himself in my shoes to understand my pains and gains. He then matched my preference for visualisation to his video story and then, he acted quickly to build fast trust. He realised that any time delay would erode my retention no matter how relevant his solution might be. How often have you gone back to a prospect days later and sensed the 'shine has gone' off the conversation? Speed matters here.

When we receive stories at the surface level, we get infor-mation in bite-sized pieces that we unconsciously bookmark or discard. But when a story excites us, our computer size brains fire up more of our cerebral cortex, allowing us to make analogies and inferences about our situation. And when this happens, the storyteller has a wonderful chance to influence the other person's thinking by tapping the critical, analytical, and empathetic juices hidden inside. Psychologist Doctor Uri Hasson suggests, *"by simply telling a story, (a person) could plant ideas, thoughts, and emotions into the listener's brains. A story is the only way to activate parts in the brain so that a listener turns the story into their idea and experience."* [124]

Jade was ten when I met her over 20 years ago. I was volunteering to help rehabilitate young children from challenging backgrounds. Jade arrived with little more than the clothes on her back and a toothbrush for a week. She slept, showered, and swam in the same clothes for the duration of that week. There is much more to Jade's story, and it left a lasting impact on me.

Fast forward 20 years, back at university, I realised not much had happened in terms of access and inclusion to opportunities for young people. I was shocked. With Jade's story still etched in my mind and supported by global scientific research, I launched Exit Entry in 2019. An initiative to measure the skills and interests of students to connect them with college and work opportunities. We have now seen over 60,000 students on the platform and over twenty million engagements through our social channels.

The journey has just started. Understanding and supporting students is paramount to creating equal access to learning,

development, and opportunities. Jade's story inspired me back then and is helping me today to help others.
Lewize McCauley Crothers, CEO & Founder, Exit Entry

Consider the times you have been excited about a potential opportunity and put in the long hours producing your best compelling value proposition, only never to hear back from the other person. Admit it. We have all had that experience. Is it because we misjudged the initial contact with the other person and failed to capture their genuine issues? Did we not mix a strong enough cocktail to excite, arouse and bond with them? Or did we simply fail to think about the frequency they would be on when receiving our story?

When did you last consider the person, you hoped to influence? Or do you use the default storytelling approach every time? Presenting to an audience, you will want to control the narrative, but when in a one-to-one conversation, why not ask the question *'how is it best to share my thoughts with you?* I have often heard customers ask for a bullet point email or even text message because they travel and prefer that portrait experience whilst queuing for a plane. I have had others who would like a WhatsApp voice message to give the bare bones of the proposition so they can listen to it while doing their weekend 5k. A story that they can consume on their terms, not the storytellers.

Which one are you?

Are you a storyteller or a story thinker? Or both? The former is where we share a narrative with someone else, where the content might be our original work or that produced by others around us. The latter is when we consciously stop to consider who the audience is, what the message is, their situation, and what the story will make them think, feel, say, and do - and tap into their pains and gains. Sounds quite different or is the same thing?

In business we should be able to tell better stories. As human beings We have the computational jelly between our ears - apparently enough to wrap around the planet four times. And we have all the words from our purpose and value statements, product descriptions and unique selling propositions. But I maintain just having a story to tell is not enough. Before we can tell a good story we have to think about the story we are going to tell. Shoot me down for stating the obvious but I am not sure this is always the case. How is this for you and others around you? Not just the words but also how we will deliver the message and how we connect to our audience.

It's the way he tells them

In drafting this book I fell into many of the traps of a first-time writer, namely procrastination, indulgence, and verbosity. What if I had written blogs instead? Turning this book into a blog series would have given me enough content to publish an article weekly for up to half a year. Or as a weekly podcast with my guest contributors. Or not bother at all and keep the anecdotes as stories when I meet people?

When we are asked to tell a story too often we converge

on the preparation and delivery, *'how do my slides look,'* *'have I got enough razzmatazz on the visuals?'* or, in my case, *'have I written enough?'* I know I write too much! But It is unlikely we are employed as story writers so the content we are using for the story is often someone else's handiwork, where interpretation is the differentiator. You and I can both be given the same slides or storyline and come at it completely differently.

In the finite game where competition is high, the presentation can bizarrely take precedence over whether our story stacks up. I recall many a battle with marketing colleagues more interested in whether I had my slides ready for a up-coming event and not whether my content conveyed a compelling message. I will admit I was an awkward colleague at times because I rarely had my slides ready. I would be somewhere else focused on how my story would translate to the audience which explains the last-minute panic to conform to the rules! Do you agree that unless we are tuned into the audience's frequency, it wouldn't matter if we had the best-looking material ever produced or not?

We are all in the audience at some point in our lives - at the theatre or annual corporate event. We sit there trying to simplify and organise what we are seeing and hearing into our wavelength, but if we can't we get tired, and check out eventually. And whilst the presenter or actor might think they are doing a great job, their use of audio and visual can be 'too busy' for the audience to keep up. And I don't mean flashing lights. And when the addition of numbers is taken into account the pressure on our audience to spin plates can be counterproductive.

Storytelling by numbers

We love telling stories with numbers. All quite necessary to gain support for ideas and solutions we are chasing, but as Daniel Kahneman's points out, *"no one ever made a decision because of a number. They need a story."* [125] In the finite game though, a good set of numbers is like the entry pass to a club. Without such you are not getting in. I have often wondered that one of the reasons behind 'a good set of numbers' is because the presenter is playing with me. Once you show me a good set of numbers it shuts off my ability to reason and ask you to explain what your number means. Like a smokescreen. And before you say, 'that's not me,' consider your daily ritual of business as usual how many 'numbers' do you handle without having a story to underpin what you are being asked to understand. And I mean really understand.

Are we guilty of forgoing a human-centric character storyline because we think it will obfuscate our neat numerical plot-based proposition? The finite game that we play as Convergers is only interested in the story of success and a well-crafted spreadsheet can be the best story ever. An approach aimed at reducing complexity, uncertainty and doubt for our audience. Yes, we may couple human stories to our pitches, but we don't invest the time in making them flow with drama, protagonists, and their outcomes. Why bother with that? Instead, we will focus heavily on our visualisations and soundbites to convince the audience we are on their side. A form of trust relationship that depending on the audience might be absolutely fine. But what if it isn't? And the person opposite is showing signs of signs of disappointment or worse.

What if there was a way to use numbers in our storytelling that makes the connection we need to achieve. How might we use numbers to help us convey our message in a way that is powerful and direct?

Three is one such number

In Western society, we have a thing about the number three. Our clothes are either small, medium, or large, we eat three meals a day and obey traffic lights of three colours. And in writing, it is considered *"that a trio of events or characters is more humorous, satisfying, or effective than other numbers."* [126] Even at the core of being human, the atom consists of three parts, and our existence on earth has a beginning, a middle and an end. And as children, we are told fairy tales and nursery rhymes that adhere to this preference for things in three. I share this because one of the biggest challenges in business we face is over-indulgence in telling stories.

Sit through a corporate presentation and be prepared to be drowned in content beautifully laid out in attractive colours and artistic animation. But because of the firehose effect of not being able to turn off the information flow, we are often left hours later with messy disconnected snippets in our heads. Attending a conference, especially the recent online versions, can be an overwhelming experience of information rush. But unless something dramatic happens in what we hear from the countless speakers, anything we thought we had learned loses fidelity and context after a short while. Our brains might be incredibly complex organs, but the reality is that we can only retain a small amount of information simultaneously, gravitating to rely on short, memorable patterns that are easier to recount. It is exhausting, and we just don't like it that much. This is why the Power of Three is an interesting frame for your storytelling approach.

Point Story Point

Imagine you have a story to tell. You know the subject well and have your evidence and critical points mapped out. You are just about to reach for your default delivery mechanism, be it PowerPoint, blog, tweet, LinkedIn post or podcast. But before you do start by asking yourself these three questions.

- What is the single most important point of view (PoV) that amplifies my story the best?
- What is the drama and who is the protagonist that is relevant to my audience?
- Will my story change the situation for my audience? Why should they care?

The questions are designed to challenge you to think about three aspects of what you are about to say. Well of course you do, because if we are selling something we will have plenty to go along with, and if we are buying, we won't be too far behind on that score. But when I ask you to think of the most important point of view did you find that quite easy to do? Or do you have several you want to put across in your story? Trust me we are pretty poor at being able to articulate our main point of view. Instead, we tend to feel we need to 'gild the lily' and pile more on top.

Then ask yourself how relevant is your chosen <u>STORY</u> that amplifies this chosen point of view. An example that is not only relevant to your point of view but also contains sufficient drama that will resonate with the person receiving your words. Yes, drama. You have to find something that triggers their hormone release. And I don't mean fabricating your story because if you do then I can't help you. Do you have an abundance of examples that you find hard to find just one which I am asking you to do? And is your example more plot-centric than human-centric? Do you emphasise in your story what's at stake for the audience -the loss or gain, success, or failure - of something important to them? I often see a strong point of view undone because of an irrelevant or confusing choice of supporting the story.

And lastly, does your final <u>POINT</u> make a clear connection with the other person by describing what it means to them? Some will say 'call 'call to action' or 'compelling reason to act.' Others will say 'what this means to you is....' Either way, you need to give a clear and concise signal to the audience that there is something they need to do. I know, I know - signalling is Sales 101 stuff but I had to say it!

The important thing here is that your story disrupts them sufficiently to think about their situation and whether you - your company and product - can help them improve it. This is Point Story Point. A tip I am humbly indebted to Isobel Rimmer, a respected management coach, who explained it to me a few years ago. I call it my Swiss Army knife to help me prise open the structure of a story I am about to tell.

Concise does it

Consider this tweet *"This is not life as usual. There is a density in New York City that is destructive. It has to stop, and it has to stop now. New York City must develop an immediate plan to reduce density."* [127]

Using Point Story Point it breaks down like this.

- *"This not life as usual"* - the opening point of view. This was different. Out of the ordinary.
- *"There is a density in New York City that is destructive. It has to stop, and it has to stop now"* - containing the drama suggesting something bad is happening and if we don't do something about it things will get worse.
- *"New York City must develop an immediate plan to reduce density"*. The call to action says, 'we need to do something about this right away.'

When I first read it I visualised footage of chiller trucks in the street acting as temporary morgues, thinking about people living in those neighbourhoods with their fears and hopes. It also made me think of my situation, given we too, in the UK, were facing the same humanitarian crisis. If this was happening in New York, why not my home town? The author of the tweet, Mayor Cuomo had cleverly shaken up the cocktail of emotion to write words that would make his audience think. All done in less than 140 characters.

This powerful story made a character-based connection with me, directly firing up my hormones to feel a mix of fear, shock, and self-preservation. Cuomo was sharing an auditory and visual experience through his words. And when this happened, I gave his message my full attention. We all remember another American politician adept at using similar tactics but perhaps with less thought attached to the message!

Mayor Cuomo was a story thinker. He had thought of his audience, structured his story, and chose a platform that would get them to react. When was the last time you thought about writing a tweet to describe your 'killer story'? Our stories will not likely be so life critical but that doesn't mean they are not entitled to be given some thought. And a well-crafted story, even a tweet, can be all it takes to fire up hormones in the other person to want to have a conversation with you.

Hint

Think about a proposition or idea you are working on. Maybe you are building a sales campaign, building up a business case to seek funding for an idea you have or tackling an argument you are involved in. Start with a blank piece of paper and write down the word POINT. Now consider the one point of view you want to transmit to the audience. Now write down the word STORY. Consider the drama or tension behind your point of view. It might be something about to change in the audience's world or a growing problem that might be around the corner for them. Be mindful of making this character based and not too abstract. Think of someone affected by the issue you are considering. And then write down the word POINT again.

Now it is your chance to tell the audience there is something they need to do about it. Their call to action. The action side of your story is because you need to get a reaction, outcome, or result. Keep in mind the phrase *'so what does this means to them.'* Do not worry if you struggle at first; just keep practising. And share it with others. Make it something your team can try when working on a story for a bid presentation or when asked to put forward ideas for consideration in management events.

Point story point is just a tactic. A tactic to disrupt how we view the stories we tell. It isn't a wonder drug or panacea to successfully story writing, but it is a frame to help you. In your world, you might be surrounded by so much information that you drown in trying to get across your message concisely. So just like the Empathy Map and Stop Start Better, the use of Point Story Point is another tool in the Diverger's toolkit for you to experiment with.

In business, our stories have to communicate our position on the matter at hand - our point of view. Otherwise, people won't know what we stand for, and they won't understand why we do what we do. Consider how you would respond to being asked *'so tell me your point of view on ethical sustainability for ACME Plc product lifecycle.'* I would hope your answer would be the same as the CEO but who knows? Does it have to be? Either way, we all need clarity on our point of view whether it is *'our product is a hundred times better than our competitors'* or *'the world will be better off when we stop using single-use plastic.'*

The power of low fidelity

When we listen to music we tend to develop an ear for high-quality output and performance. This search for high audio output levels will deter us from anything that sounds imperfect, tinny, and low fidelity - for example, soundproof headsets on aeroplanes versus the ones you get for £1. Or in business when shown visualisations of performance and results using graphs and animation versus the 'back of a cigarette packet' scribble on a pad.

The customer pleaded, "what if I could just get a sticky note on my screen every morning with the numbers I need to run my business? If I got that, I would be a happy man." This was 20 years ago, and the customer was a senior leader in a high street bank, surrounded by every conceivable slice-and-dice dashboard. Yet no one had asked him what insight was 'simply good enough.'

They had assumed they knew the answer, so they did not bother asking the question. My business kicked on from that story as we wrestled with the power of data and analytics and the human ability to consume what they saw on the screen. This is why I have always paused discussions about Big Data and information transformation until we understand what matters.

When I look back over those 20 years, If put on the spot, I would say it is about how we frame questions to get under the skin of the person with the problem. Sure, data analytics is a fantastic transformation, but it is about getting it to make a true difference to someone every day and in context to their business. That is still the hardest part but the part I have enjoyed the most.

Jason Betteridge, Managing Director, Circyl

The role of play

And don't underestimate the role of play as a mechanism to explore stories. As children, we grew up using play to experience stories and through early education, a tool used by teachers to help us experience our learning. But then when we get to be 'grown up' the chances dwindle as we settle into channelled storytelling rigour.

I once spent an enlightening afternoon with a group of oil company executives with sleeves rolled up, simulating a refinery pipeline problem, using only objects found in the room - pencils, paper, water jugs, phones - and several expensive ties! A visualisation exercise that removed the noise usually attributed to such high-brow sessions, through the use of play, cranked open the problem in a way never previously thought.

I came up with a game of my own - the smartphone game. It is not super unique and probably won't be a keeper, but I have used it at times to help people synthesise what is important to them. Let me explain.

When people are talking about a new piece of innovation or a problem they need to solve, I would ask them to draw around their phone on a piece of card. I would then ask them to cut out their 'smartphone' with scissors and then stand up and walk to the other side of the room holding their 'smartphone.' In silence, I would ask them to consider as they walked, *'what three things would you need on your phone to inform you that the new idea is working.'* I would ask them to write down in silence their three things. The only rule was that it had to be three things - not one, fifteen or seventy-six. And it couldn't also be 'popular apps' i.e., Facebook, email, and Zoom. No, it could only be three pieces of information they needed to know to help them understand their transformation project i.e., a progression number (financial or otherwise), a video stream of an object, and a clock showing the time used so far.

And then I would ask them to compare their phones with each other to see who matched and who didn't. The exercise was not about getting them all to be the same - that would be self-defeating, wouldn't it? Or would it? That's a debate for another time. No, the aim of the smartphone game was to get them to think and pause their natural urge to want more. A way to frame their thinking around just three things using the metaphor of the smartphone as a way to challenge them.

Stories told using data

Increasingly we rely on data to give our conversation clarity and to provide an empirical way to inform decisions. People prefer presenting data because it is seen as clean and factual, whilst words are messy, subjective, and open to interpretation. This is why we try so hard in business to convert stories into data-driven stories to make out points logically and directly and to remove ambiguity. And when we use the power of data in our stories, we really can shift entire mindsets along the path towards *'believing what is on the screen.'* I particularly recall the saying *"data is the new oil,"* attributed to Clive Humby of Tesco.[128] Soon awestruck audiences were confronted with what was fast becoming a data storytelling revolution. It felt at times that just saying your story was a data-led story was enough to win people over. Why target human emotions when I can hit you hard with every slice-and-dice analysis available that appeals to your logical brain?

And now 'data skill' is present in more jobs than ever. In every facet of public and private life, we look at everything in absolute terms - progress to target, performance to budget, and effort against goals. We do this because data help us convince others through the clean lines of numbers and facts, that we can deliver predictable results and successful outcomes to them i.e., *our product is X times faster than theirs, and using our service can save you year on year X percentage* and so on.

Give me a button

When I see a button I am increasingly attracted to the designer of not only what is written on the button but on what might happen if I press it. I will ponder how accurate is the button's stated purpose to what really will happen. Of course, this has led me to press buttons that don't work as designed and leave me quite frustrated. And don't ask me about car park machines.

A button to press is the metaphor for intrigue and curiosity. We are told not to press buttons we don't understand but we can't help ourselves. Look at how cybercriminals exploit the button (URL link) on SMS scam messages. Or the button display in a modern car. Exploiting this human bias to 'see what happens' explains why companies industrialise button design. And one wonders whether the US President's nuclear football button work as designed? Can you imagine what is written on that particular button - *'Go? Wait 5 minutes? I'm so sorry.'*

I love my financial portal. It gives me everything I need to know. I have a financial advisor who professionally helps me with context and reasons why things are this way and that. Do I understand what I can see? Not often is my honest answer but what else can I be shown to make me more knowledgeable? What if I could press a button that connected me to stories of people 'like me'? People with similar financial portfolios and outlooks on pensions, risk, and investments? Like a Dollar Street (excuse the pun) for financial storytelling. A 'people like me button' might seem crazy and impractical to the financial folk but it was just an idea.

Think before data speaks

Can we infer what we need to share with someone else if all we communicate is a 'number'? Or do we need context behind the digit on our screen to make the point? If I whisper to you *'it is number 8'* it will mean little, but if we are standing at Heathrow e-gates looking for the next available passport scanner it might be good information.

And whilst this is part and parcel of how humans communicate, we are increasingly left with just numbers and scant storytelling to help us. It is as if the numbers (because they are presented nicely) will do the trick. Social media is an excellent platform to share whatever we want but too often numbers and soundbites leave us wanting more.

Consider this. You have a meeting where your task is to present progress against a goal you are working on. Nothing to see here, right? A data-rich environment that is as granular as you want it. A task characterised by a robust-looking template of graphs and numbers showing quarterly sales forecast, monthly opportunity pipeline and annual budget planning predictions. We all know about these sorts of meetings and charts - quite logical and devoid of any character-based plot. Deliberately so. No one wants to mix in subjective and squidgy human stories. A bit like using a knife covered in jam to spread the marmalade. Who does that? But this time you do something slightly different. Just before you open up your first numbers slide you show the room a <u>Story Page</u>. A page that explains what is coming next through your data, by connecting to a human story impacted by the figures to be shown subsequently. A page that has a plot, drama, protagonist and question - the foundations of a good story.

Stories disrupt

If your story doesn't stop the other person in their tracks then your opportunity has been lost. Think about that for a second. How often do we pitch a story without realising the other person is not listening to us?

Story thinking is about being disruptive. It is about building your story up with the audience in mind and selecting the best medium to connect with them. It is about not just thinking about the words but also the other person. Story thinking can be messy and unpredictable. But don't worry because our brains are prepared for such disarray.

To be a story thinker doesn't require extensive coaching or qualifications. But it does require to develop a habit to think about the person receiving your story; like Anna Rosling Rönnlund or Thinking Guy. And when you do you will open up possibilities about how to share your story. Story thinking is fun to do, and we can all do it - whether we choose a tweet, a corporate presentation or even a book to tell our stories. Story thinking is about finding a way to disrupt the other person and to make them tune in. As Seth Godin says, *"People do not buy goods and services. They buy relations, stories, and magic."* [129]

Recap

Our business-as-usual approach is all about winning the finite game we are playing. As a result, we can often be trapped in a trilogy of temptations. And while this happens the infinite game of uncertainty and complexity that we just have to keep playing no matter what challenges us to keep up. And when we get too immersed in doing what we think is right - our Converger self - we miss the chance to pause and ask, *'is there a better way.'*

I have spoken about the landscape of today that suggests volatility, uncertainty, complexity, and ambiguity (VUCA) will challenge us to think differently. A time when our strategy will increasingly focus on Outcome to work backwards through the DBOFO framework - design, build operate, function and outcome.

To be a Diverger takes courage. Not courage with a C, but the courage to stop and be more inquisitive about the other person and the help we can give them. As Dag Hammarskjöl, a Swedish economist wrote, *"It is when we all play safe that we create a world of utmost insecurity. It is when we all play safe that fatality will lead us to our doom. It is in the dark shade of courage alone that the spell can be broken."*[130]

CHAPTER 8

EVEN IF IT WAS FREE

*"The most exciting breakthroughs of the 21st century will
not occur because of technology but because of an
expanding concept of what it means to be human."*
- JOHN NAISBITT

Even if 'it' (technology) had been free he was not going to
sign. At the time we might have thought Free Guy was
being reckless or obstructive, but the truth was he was
being courageous. He wasn't the problem, we were. And
despite what we say, it is hard being wrong or as Joshua
Rothman puts it *"the real challenge isn't being right but
knowing how wrong you might be."* [131]

While Free Guy spoke from his gut, we were speaking with
our heads. The conversation might as well be conducted in
different languages for all the empathy in the room that
day. He was thinking about outcomes for his people; we

were thinking about compensation and our next deal. We had a deal to close so why should we stop and help Free Guy reframe his problem? Let the buyer beware, right? It couldn't be our fault that he had doubts. He had asked the question to the marketplace, and we had answered it - better than anyone else. Just sign the contract Free Guy! Yet we were the ones leaving the room with an unsigned deal and a 'baying mob' back at base wanting to know why.

Press me to diverge

What if we could? A button we could take into meetings, workshops, and other conversations that when pressed would quickly rewire our brains just long enough to turn on our Diverger's mindset. And if we had this button what would that do to how we looked at problems and solutions? A button that doesn't look at the logical and analytical side of the opportunity but figures out the emotional and irrational side of the human being the other side. A button that could have warned me that Free Guy was going to push back the way he did. A button that would challenge the trilogy of temptations by asking ourselves whether we are being too confident, too smart, and too biased in our approach to the conversation. Of course, this is not reality, but it does make you think, right?

VUCA is not going away

I won't apologise for saying this again. Our lives today are immersed in VUCA - volatility, uncertainty, complexity, and ambiguity. Not in a dystopian way, but in a grounded view of the bumps in the road that seem to be less spaced apart than before. A space where trust appears to be at an all-time low depending on your perspective. And let's not forget the words of those CEOs who complained, *"we try to match complexity with greater complexity and speed with increased speed. Feeling out of control, we seek more control. Instead of the clarity we crave, we get ambiguity and more uncertainty."*

Space to matter

This book has not been about technology. It has been about us. It has been about how we conduct ourselves in the conversations we have when discussing problems and solutions increasingly helped by 'technology.' A conversation that sees us swap our Converger and Diverger mindsets without being aware of what we are doing. A conversation that stretches our ability to retain the finite game of winning- sales and buying - with an ever-increasing realisation that we need to address purposeful human outcomes much more.

This might seem as common sense as night and day but in the words of Victor E Frankl, psychologist and Holocaust survivor, speak strongly, *"between stimulus and response, there is a space. In that space is our power to choose our response. In our response lies our growth and our freedom."* [132]

Every day we strive to find space. Whether it is to think clearer, reduce our stress levels or discover what is important versus what is not. But space is a limited resource itself. And in a business world powered by technological innovation that breeds the confidence for us to do agile things we should have more space not less to think about our next problem or opportunity. But it just doesn't seem to work out that way. Whether it is our productivity that seems to be compromised or the inability of teams to create a stronger trust to work together to help others, our ability to manage space to think is under threat.

Convergence is inevitable. Divergence is optional

We have created a world where the Converger mindset dominates. A world where logic and science trump emotion and curiosity. A world that can talk about magic and excitement but only if conforming against a landscape of business models, measurable processes, and certainty of outcome. It is how humankind as a species survives, sensing danger and reacting unconsciously to design our way out of trouble. It is why we fare better than any other species - for now at least. But being a Converger is tiring shutting down our human credentials for creative ideas and imaginative ways to find better ways to help ourselves.

As leaders, we set out the pitch for the game dictating the tactics and monitoring progress to target. We will encourage creativity to a point but are wary that too much diverse thought hurts the number and risks losing the game. The irony is that we will happily devote time to 'qualification' without ever questioning the merit and outcome involved.

Rediscover our inner Diverger

When we diverge we seek opinions outside of our comfort

zone, encouraging us to be vulnerable to not knowing the answer and avoiding rushing in with the answer. When we diverge, we find the missing bullet holes, spot the mother-in-law, and invent the windscreen wiper.

This is why being a Diverger is so important. All of us at some point will meet Free Guy. Someone who challenges our view of the world as the ultimate cynic. Someone desperate for us to help them understand their problem space better, challenge them with deeper questions and share stronger stories of where we can help the most.

Let me ask you if you saw an advert for a Diverger, would you apply? Of course, it is unlikely you will see such an advert because employers believe they are implicitly recruiting people with these skills already. I don't have any data to share but I wonder if this is the case how long does it take for someone to 'forget' their Diverger skillset?

In my travels I have met many Divergers, some helped me write this book. Whilst they don't have the word Diverger stuck to their foreheads nor in their job profiles, they out-wardly display a willingness and humility to inquire deeply and display vulnerability when trying to understand and help others. If they were members of a club - *'Club Diverge'* - they would be the happiest experimenting and exploring problems, sharing stories of successes (and failures) to broaden the minds of fellow members. And the thing with Club Diverge is that we are all members. There is no entrance policy. Jeans, trainers, and an open mind are allowed. Cynics too.

Diverger's toolkit

The hints are just that - hints. Tools that I have tried and had successes and failures with. A mixed bag that will not change your world overnight but might help you develop a Diverger's mindset through the habits you follow. I treat this as an experiment because I am continually testing and retesting and hope you will share your thoughts with me.

If you were to press me to pick out one tool you should think about, I suggest you think about how you go about asking <u>beautiful questions</u>. Not in terms of flowery wordsmithing or Shakespearian prose, but in terms of simplicity and curiosity. You may find you are already using this 'tool' in your way which is fine. But like any tool, there is a chance of 'rust' so think of the beautiful question as a spray of WD40! Either way, we can all benefit from a dose of humility to say to ourselves *'I don't think I know enough about the problem nor the person I think who has it.'* So forgive me to cover the 5Ws again.

- **What is?** Have we challenged known facts, assumptions and biases about the problem or the space the problem is occupying?
- **Who has?** Do we know who really does have the problem and how well have we captured their feelings, thoughts, pains, and gains on the problem discussed?
- **What if?** Have we reframed the problem to see if there is a better idea that is missing? Have we created a way to allow everyone to feel their ideas have value and are we able to iterate ideas until we

find our strongest candidate?

- **What wows?** Have we over-egged our solution with too much focus on what we believe is 'smart' but not on what is desirable, feasible and viable for the person with the problem?
- **What works?** When ideas gather momentum from the initial concept, how well does the idea stack up when told in the context of the intended environment (system of systems)? Remember DBOFO? Have we loaded our attention on the design-build and function at the expense of the operation and outcome?

And think about the 5W stories I have shared in this book.

- Procurement Woman who prompted people to ask, 'what is...' going on in Singapore.
- The aid agency in Bangladesh assumed 'who has...' when helping expectant mothers.
- Mary Anderson asked 'what if...' while watching the driver clear the snow off the tramcar window.
- Suzi Lu asked 'what wows...' when prototyping the visualised receipt.
- The NASA team figured out 'what works...' when helping the Apollo crew return to earth.

Free Guy

But Is his story an example of bygone years that have been superseded by the tight connection between technology, outcome and growth? Has the use of agile in every sense removed these 'old-fashioned' fears? Or does it speak to the truth, that despite the abundance of technology we are still prone to misjudge what we believe to be so? Did this contradiction in terms - 'even if it was free' - portray a deeper conversation needed as we unquestionably travel faster in our decision making helped by the tech we crave for?

Where are we headed

In the words of American author William Gibson, *"the future is here, it's just not evenly distributed."* [133]And if you subscribe to the VUCA world still being with us for the foreseeable, then we are all going to need to exercise our Diverger mindset a lot more. Why? We are increasingly attributing our successes to the technology we buy, rather than the guile and endeavour of the human behaviour affected. Such thinking of course plays well for the increased role of technology and those selling. And to the experts who confidently draw boxes around human problems and transform them into technical solutions. But what if our problems are not easily programmable for Tobi and Terri when the landscape is so turbulent and complex? How might we counterbalance our urge to go faster with a sense of doing what is best even if that means we have to slow down first?

My description of converger and diverger might appear too abstract to many. The cut and thrust of business life do not lend itself easily to having moments to consciously stop to diverge on how we approach our problems. Life doesn't work that way, does it? Our brains are not designed that way, and neither are the businesses we work for. No matter how hard we try. And the answer? It is out there, somewhere, but it will take a delicious concoction of what we think we know and what we don't. It will take us to bring both our converger and diverger mindset to the table and be mindful of what this means to others sitting with us. An honest and open admission that confronts this slice of wisdom, *'if you think technology is the answer to your problems, then you neither understand technology nor your problems.'*

When we diverge we will get better at solving problems through inclusive design that is thoughtful, considered, and all-embracing, designed for everyone's needs, not for the people we think has the problem.

My Dad is eighty-nine and suffers from Dementia. We want to try and keep him in his own home for as long as possible as we feel this is the best place for him. So we bought him a 'smart' TV. Is there any other type nowadays? All my dad wants to watch is snooker and old films. But he could not operate it himself with all the buttons and hundreds of channels, so we got him a 'Big Button' controller to make it workable for him and reduce the times when he lost 'the telly.'

The irony is that the answer came from removing the 'smart' for which we had paid - probably extra as well. The TV cannot help him with his love for Perry Como without a convoluted intervention by the family and smartphones, so we got him a 'simple red box,' not a smart one. A box that my dad can operate himself. Sometimes, his memory 'forgets' the difference between the phone, the TV remote, and the red box, creating upset and confusion for him.

Entertainment for my Dad is fragile, and I wish it were not. He is one of the millions of people with similar and more pressing needs, and yet 'smart' things do not seem to be designed for people like my Dad. I can only guess it was intended for someone else. How is that possible? In hindsight, if someone had offered me the Smart TV for free, I would firmly say no thanks. But if I could pay each day for what I think is a fair price for my dad to hum along to Perry and watch his snooker, I would think about that.

Catherine Russell, Daughter

That's it. But before you go I do want to leave this sentence with you - *'just because you can (ideas, money, investors), doesn't mean you should (resources, machines, materials) unless you know why (purpose, ethics, outcomes).'* My book has been about how when we converge we often fail to connect these words successfully, but when we diverge - we can't half do a brilliant job!

The End.

Thank you
for taking the time to read my
book.

If you are curious to learn more use the QR code
below to book a call with me.

Email - paul@evenifitwasfree.biz

Even if it was free

Even if it was free

ACKNOWLEDGMENTS

I honestly did not realise how hard it is to write a book. I do now and have a few people to thank for helping me over the last year to get across the line.

Joseph Sanderton for encouraging me to explore the design thinking philosophy in Stockholm, Lindsey Moore for her kind peer review, Luan Wise for her wise counsel, Emma Cowley for her design skills and Michael Estrada for his invaluable support at the eleventh hour. A nod to past IBM colleagues for their commitment and humour - Sue Bohane, Paul Gatland, Kylie Jones, Priesh Kamani, Rebecca Calthorpe, Joe Korting and Nils Van Der Zijl. To my loyal friends at Servo and URS and across the Microsoft PAC community for their unswerving support and friendship. To the pandemic Design Thinkers Group who helped build something special during the lockdown. And to Mark Bew for allowing me to see the other side of the conversation.

Finally, this book would not have been possible without the support of my wonderful children - Sam, Joe, and Alice. And to my wife, Cathy, a special thank you for your encourage-ment and incredible patience as I no doubt drove you mad with my pleas of *'one more edit, I promise.'*

P.S. Free Guy did eventually sign the deal - and not for free.

It turns out we are all in sales!

Even if it was free

REFERENCES

ABOUT THE TITLE
[1]https://www.goodreads.com/quotes/104892-to-look-at-something-as-though-we-had-never-seen
[2]https://news.gallup.com/businessjournal/14503/what-were-they-thinking.aspx

Chapter 1- A TRILOGY OF TEMPTATIONS
[3]https://bit.ly/3ByylNY
[4]https://7lafa.com/lyricsen/346374
[5]https://hasler.ece.gatech.edu/Published_papers/Technology_overview/gordon_moore_1965_article.pdf
[6]https://bit.ly/3KCVbb6
[7]https://bit.ly/34UTPsy
[8]https://www.ibm.com/blogs/nordic-msp/mayflowers-ai-captain/
[9]https://www.youtube.com/watch?v=m6U9T3R3EQg&t=1501s
[10]https://bit.ly/3KCV13u
[11]https://bit.ly/3LYaH1A
[12]Mnemonic: Sentences to Remember the Order of the Planets (ict4us.com)
[13]https://www.bbc.co.uk/news/science-environment-33462184
[14]https://www.discovermagazine.com/planet-earth/7-groundbreaking-ancient-civilizations-that-influence-us-today
[15]https://www.goodreads.com/quotes/76778-business-and-human-endeavors-are-systems-we-tend-to-focus-on
[16]https://thedecisionlab.com/biases/the-sunk-cost-fallacy
[17]https://thedecisionlab.com/insights/health/stress-redesigns-decision-making
[18]https://www.zdnet.com/article/does-it-matter-now/
[19]https://www.linkedin.com/pulse/porter-m-e-1996-what-

strategy-harvard-business-review-salman-siddiqui/

[20]Alan Turing: The experiment that shaped artificial intelligence - BBC News

[21]https://www.newyorker.com/tech/annals-of-technology/ada-lovelace-the-first-tech-visionary

[22] https://en.wikipedia.org/wiki/CAPTCHA

[23] https://www.britannica.com/technology/Jacquard-loom

[24]https://99percentinvisible.org/episode/the-eliza-effect/

Chapter 2- SEDUCED BY CONFIDENCE

[25]https://skeptics.stackexchange.com/questions/22375/did-a-soviet-nail-factory-produce-useless-nails-to-improve-metrics

[26]https://simonsinek.com/podcast-episodes/the-infinite-game-with-dr-james-carse/

[27] https://wtf.tw/ref/carse.pdf

[28]https://en.wikipedia.org/wiki/Scientific_management

[29]https://www.forbes.com/sites/blakemorgan/2022/08/09/i-feel-supported-by-managementunited-flight-attendants-rate-their-bosses-via-nps/?sh=638564854fbc

[30]https://b.gatech.edu/3jxD1eW

[31]https://bit.ly/3wYafKV

[32]https://en.wikipedia.org/wiki/Goodhart%27s_law

[33]https://www.nature.com/articles/d41586-020-02009-w

[34]https://www.raconteur.net/technology/artificial-intelligence/hannah-fry-ditch-crap-science-and-get-real-about-what-ai-can-do/

[35]https://www.nytimes.com/2013/03/03/opinion/sunday/the-perils-of-perfection.html

[36]https://www.theguardian.com/technology/2014/feb/19/google-glass-advice-smartglasses-glasshole

[37]https://www.princeofwales.gov.uk/speech/speech-hrh-prince-wales-150th-anniversary-royal-institute-british-architects-riba-royal-gala

[38]https://www.gartner.com/en/documents/3956304/how-

markets-and-vendors-are-evaluated-in-gartner-magic-q
[39]https://www.gartner.co.uk/en/methodologies/gartner-hype-cycle
[40]https://www.mcgill.ca/oss/article/general-science/tips-better-thinking-surviving-only-half-story
[41]https://twitter.com/TimHarford/status/13184359792928 23557?s=20&t=fAmNoB-0_AXOl2k6ZdVU_g
[42]https://med.stanford.edu/news/all-news/2012/07/stanford-medicine-magazine-examines-sciences-deluge-of-big-data.html
[43]https://medium.com/ethnography-matters/why-big-data-needs-thick-data-b4b3e75e3d7

CHAPTER 3 - INNOVATE OR DIE
[44]https://www.wired.co.uk/article/startup-of-the-week-what3words
[45]https://bit.ly/3KvvpW9
[46]https://www.tvlicensing.co.uk/cs/media-centre/news/view.app?id=1369787209230
[47]https://www.geekwire.com/2012/robbie-bachs-lessons-intrapreneurship-xbox-zune/
[48]https://www.thersa.org/blog/2017/07/from-design-think-ing-to-system-change
[49]https://en.wikipedia.org/wiki/Who_Moved_My_Cheese%3F
[50]https://www.hrzone.com/lead/culture/why-did-google-abandon-20-time-for-innovation
[51]https://www.hrzone.com/lead/culture/why-did-google-abandon-20-time-for-innovation
[52]https://www.forbes.com/profile/traviskalanick/?sh=4e25 39c36199
[53]https://www.statista.com/statistics/301669/number-of-licensed-taxis-in-england-and-wales-uk/
[54]https://www.vodafone.com/about-vodafone/what-we-do/consumer-products-and-services/m-pesa

[55]https://digitaltonto.com/2017/the-30-years-rule-innovation-takes-a-lot-longer-than-you-think/

[56]https://www.mckinsey.com/business-functions/people-and-organizational-performance/our-insights/agility-it-rhymes-with-stability

[57]https://bit.ly/3veAP1b

[58]https://hbswk.hbs.edu/item/clay-christensens-milkshake-marketing

[59]https://career.uconn.edu/blog/2015/09/01/change-is-inevitable-growth-is-optional/

[60]https://www.linkedin.com/pulse/chapter-two-four-zones-geoffrey-moore/

[61]https://www.harvard.co.uk/six-ideas-every-pr-professional-know/

[62]https://www.cnbc.com/2019/10/14/jeff-bezos-this-is-the-smartest-thing-we-ever-did-at-amazon.html

[63]http://www.archive.8m.net/huxley.htm

[64]https://thedecisionlab.com/biases/functional-fixedness

[65]https://trustedadvisor.com/why-trust-matters/understanding-trust/understanding-the-trust-equation

[66] https://www.tablegroup.com/pat/

CHAPTER 4 - GO FASTER, SLOWLY

[67] Can We Gain Strength From Shame?". "TED Radio Hour" with Guy Raz, www.npr.org. March 11, 2013.

[68]https://www.youtube.com/watch?v=k5eL_al_m7Q

[69]https://www.theguardian.com/commentisfree/2022/feb/15/post-office-scandal-workers-computer-system

[70]https://www.newyorker.com/magazine/2021/08/23/why-is-it-so-hard-to-be-rational

[71]https://www.forbes.com/2011/02/23/slow-down-speed-efficiency-leadership-managing-ccl.html?sh=43cc7eb84be1

[72]https://bit.ly/3Oag4N8

[73]https://obamawhitehouse.archives.gov/blog/2013/03/08

/empowering-all-women-reach-their-full-potential
[74]https://www.washingtonpost.com/technology/2018/11/1
6/wanted-perfect-babysitter-must-pass-ai-scan-
respectattitude/
[75]https://joiningdots.com/2018/11/28/is-the-use-of-ai-
dehumanising-behaviour/
[76]https://www.weforum.org/agenda/2018/03/rememberin
g-first-smartphone-simon-
ibm/#:~:text=Rob%20Smith,calculator%20and%20a%20sket
ch%20pad.
[77]https://www.liverpool.ac.uk/~rlawson/cycleweb.html
[78]https://www.ncbi.nlm.nih.gov/pmc/articles/PMC306290/
[79]https://archive.ph/20180320091111/http://archive.de-
fense.gov/Transcripts/Transcript.aspx?TranscriptID=2636#s
election-401.0-401.53
[80]https://longnow.org/seminars/02005/apr/08/cities-and-
time/
[81]https://hbswk.hbs.edu/archive/what-customers-want-
from-your-products
[82]https://positivepsychology.com/instant-gratification/
[83] https://www.slow-journalism.com/
[84]https://www.goodreads.com/book/show/559984.Momen
ts_of_Truth
[85]https://jamesclear.com/marginal-gains
[86]https://halgregersen.com/2015/04/28/8-habits-of-
curious-people/

Chapter 5 - FALL IN LOVE WITH PROBLEMS
[87]https://bit.ly/3E5aBSS
[88] https://growth.me/books/behave/
[89]https://www.kone.com/en/products-and-
services/advanced-people-flow-solutions/
[90]https://www.nasa.gov/feature/50-years-ago-houston-we-
ve-had-a-problem
[91]https://ssir.org/articles/entry/the_problem_with_proble

m_statements

[92]https://www.bbc.com/worklife/article/20201109-why-the-paradox-mindset-is-the-key-to-success

[93]https://www.editorx.com/shaping-design/article/nancy-douyon-interview

[94]https://bit.ly/3M2HbYC

[95]https://bit.ly/3uzjVLJ

[96]https://about.netflix.com/en

[97]https://www.fastcompany.com/90347782/the-humble-receipt-gets-a-brilliant-redesign

[98]https://www.forbes.com/sites/kevinkruse/2016/03/07/80-20-rule/

[99]https://hbr.org/2018/09/the-business-case-for-curiosity

[100]https://suebehaviouraldesign.com/kahneman-fast-slow-thinking/

[101]https://www.medicalnewstoday.com/articles/326058#No-substantial-gender-differences

[102]https://litemind.com/framing/

[103]https://amorebeautifulquestion.com/what-is-a-beautiful-question/

[104]https://www.goodreads.com/quotes/60780-if-i-had-an-hour-to-solve-a-problem-i-d

[105]https://www.consumerreports.org/car-safety/crash-test-bias-how-male-focused-testing-puts-female-drivers-at-risk/

[106]https://www.inc.com/magazine/201203/burt-helm/how-i-did-it-james-dyson.html

[107]http://ixd.prattsi.org/2016/04/disneys-magicband-the-future-of-seamless-user-experience/

[108]https://www.vice.com/en/article/g5bw3b/why-people-keep-empty-apple-iphone-macbook-boxes

[109]https://er.jsc.nasa.gov/seh/ricetalk.htm

[110]https://www.forbes.com/sites/dell/2011/11/29/business-processes-why-your-desk-is-a-dangerous-place-to-watch-the-world/?sh=47cc7b2e105e

[111]https://en.wikipedia.org/wiki/Mary_Anderson_(inventor)

#Invention_(windshield_wipers)
[112]https://hbr.org/2018/03/having-your-smartphone-nearby-takes-a-toll-on-your-thinking
[113]https://retailwire.com/discussion/ikea-tests-the-value-of-time-as-a-sales-incentive/
[114]https://www.healthline.com/health/how-long-does-it-take-to-form-a-habit#base-figure
[115]https://tinyhabits.com/book/
[116]https://www.superbetter.com/
[117]http://cs.furman.edu/~pbatchelor/mis/Slides/Porter%20Strategy%20Article.pdf
[118]http://wiredforstory.com/wired-for-story

Chapter 7 - THINK BETTER STORIES
[119]https://cmym.wordpress.com/2019/01/07/dollar-street-a-glimpse-into-how-people-live-across-the-world/
[120] https://www.youtube.com/watch?v=jGY-T4W-BOc
[121]https://www.ted.com/talks/simon_sinek_how_great_leaders_inspire_action?language=en
[122]https://bit.ly/3M6SDCo
[123]https://www.theamericanconservative.com/dreher/the-narrative-fallacy/
[124]https://bit.ly/3G08ukl
[125]https://en.wikiquote.org/wiki/Daniel_Kahneman
[126]https://en.wikipedia.org/wiki/Rule_of_three_(writing)
[127]https://twitter.com/NYGovCuomo/status/1241750717939007490?s=20&t=8hTD37OWrGU1ae9ZnTUITA
[128]https://tdwi.org/articles/2019/04/22/data-all-how-data-is-like-oil.aspx
[129]https://www.honeybook.com/risingtide/wp-content/uploads/2016/05/may.pdf
[130]*Dag Hammarskjöld, Servant of Peace*: Speeches and Statements of Dag Hammarskjöld, (1962) p107.

Chapter 8 - EVEN IF IT WAS FREE

[131]https://www.newyorker.com/magazine/2021/08/23/why-is-it-so-hard-to-be-rational

[132]https://www.viktorfrankl.org/quote_stimulus.html

[133]https://www.goodreads.com/quotes/681-the-future-is-already-here-it-s-just-not-evenly

Printed in Great Britain
by Amazon